"Christy's fearless and vulnerable st [...] your head in agreement, and silently thanking her for [...] to talk about anxiety as Christians. Full of poke-your-husband moments to 'read this, babe,' Christy makes you feel right at home. This book will help set your soul free from years of feeling guilty for feeling anxious and, instead, give you the reminder that we're all human and that God came to help us with every bit of life—the good, the bad, and the ugly."

—**Megan Swanson Rhodes,** Miss Nebraska 2014, Miss Nebraska USA 2020, CEO, Powerhouse Pageantry, and Powerhouse Collective

"Some have described anxiety as the common cold of mental illness. Today adults and young people are facing a pandemic of anxiety. With the courage of a super woman, Christy shares that she is a fellow struggler. Her candid storytelling about her debilitating anxiety and her awesome breakthrough is liberating for anyone who dares to read her book. Christy shares principles that allow the reader to leave behind the suffocating chains of anxiety."

—**Jackie Kendall,** best-selling author of *Lady in Waiting* and President of Power to Grow, Inc.

"*Nervous Breakthrough* is a must-read! Christy is honest, refreshing, and real. Though she shares her most vulnerable moments, Christy always points us back to Jesus. It's evident she is passionate about helping people break free from crippling anxiety. Thankfully, in her book, she shares the necessary tools to move us from fear to freedom."

—**Lauren Gaines,** psychologist, author, and creator of Inspired Motherhood

"In *Nervous Breakthrough*, Christy pulls the curtain back on fear, anxiety, depression, and panic, which are an epidemic in our culture. With beautiful honesty, authenticity, and sincerity, Christy shares her own painful journey. Doctors, yes. Therapy, yes. Medication, yes. Exercise, yes. Jesus, absolutely! If you are struggling, or someone you love is struggling, this is a must-read. Thank you, Christy, for your contribution to this complex subject."

—**Ron Cathcart,** lead pastor, 2Rivers Church

"In *Nervous Breakthrough*, Christy Boulware has crafted a powerful book that can serve as an antidote to anxiety attacks. She expertly combines her own experience with practical and tested advice, and she is careful to keep the reader centered on Scripture through the process. Her Ready Statements that close the book will serve as strong allies for many readers in the years to come."

—**Chris Morris,** author and mental health advocate

"What a life-changing read! I just love Christy's heart to help. As a woman who has experienced anxiety and panic attacks myself in the past, I know Christy's personal stories mixed with stats, scriptures, and encouragement are sure to help you if you're struggling with fear and anxiety. When looking for answers to overcome, as Christy wrote, 'Google is not God!' Amen to that truth!"

> —**Courtnaye Richard,** Founder of Inside Out with Courtnaye, author of *IDENTIFIED: Knowing Who You Are in Christ & Moving Forward in Your Purpose*

"The late journalist Red Smith said, 'Writing is really quite simple, all you have to do is sit down at your typewriter and open a vein.' That is exactly what Christy Boulware did in writing this book. She shares her life and her struggle with anxiety: the good and the bad, the wins and the losses, the marches forward and the steps back, sharing her experience, strength, and hope with others battling against the same demon. But this is much more than a how-to book; it's a 'who-to' book, as in who we turn to for deliverance from the pain and suffering of anxiety: God. True wholeness and healing from anxiety come in accepting the love of God in Christ Jesus. Thank you for holding up the banner of our Lord and Savior, Christy, and thanks for opening a vein."

> —**Tim Ezell,** St. Louis TV Reporter, pastor

"As you dive into the pages of this book you will receive the gift of hope and direction. Christy will help you navigate the uneasy road to your breakthrough with wisdom and practical strategies. She points to the truth found in Scripture. I especially love the way each line of the key verse is broken into practical, tangible ways to live it out and counter anxiety. I am inspired by Christy's story and admire the courage it took for her to share her story with such vulnerability. This is a life-changing book from Christy. This message is timely and will bring hope to so many hearts, including mine."

> —**Leslee Holliday,** Host of *Table Forty* Podcast, Director of Women's Ministry for Professional Athlete Outreach

"*Nervous Breakthrough* is a shining example of enduring life's test to live your testimony out loud. In this book, Christy offers poignant firsthand accounts of the reality of anxiety and panic disorder. She provides a biblical application that is both practical and informative. Boulware's experiences are so authentic and heartfelt I had no choice but to transform as the reader."

> —**Brandalyn Shropshire,** Humorist/Motivational Speaker

# NERVOUS

## BREAKTHROUGH

# NERVOUS
## BREAKTHROUGH

Finding Freedom

from Fear and Anxiety in

a World That Feeds It

CHRISTY BOULWARE

LEAFWOOD
PUBLISHERS
*an imprint of Abilene Christian University Press*

# NERVOUS BREAKTHROUGH

*Finding Freedom from Fear and Anxiety in a World That Feeds It*

LEAFWOOD
P U B L I S H E R S
*an imprint of Abilene Christian University Press*

Copyright © 2023 by Christy Boulware

978-1-68426-202-1

Printed in the United States of America

Published in association with Books & Such Literary Management, 52 Mission Circle, Suite 122, PMB 170, Santa Rosa, CA 95409-5370.

Cataloging-in-Publication Data is on file at the Library of Congress, Washington, DC.

Cover design by Thinkpen Design, LLC
Interior text design by Sandy Armstrong, Strong Design

Leafwood Publishers is an imprint of Abilene Christian University Press
ACU Box 29138 | Abilene, Texas 79699

1-877-816-4455 | www.leafwoodpublishers.com

23 24 25 26 27 28 29 / 7 6 5 4 3 2 1

# Contents

# Acknowledgments

A book never writes itself. A project of this magnitude requires a lot of time and support. When I said yes to the call to write *Nervous Breakthrough*, I had no idea the twists and turns, ups and downs that would come along with it.

I remember telling my husband that I should apply for a writing boot camp to help me with my writing career. I thought he wouldn't want me to do it because it was a hefty investment. Instead, I was greeted with great support and encouragement to take the course. That decision led me to where I am today—a first-time published author. Troy, your unwavering love and inspiration encouraged me to keep following my calling, and I wouldn't have written this book without you. I would have given up a long time ago. You sacrificed hours upon hours of parenting alone so I could focus on this mission. You are a strong tower of strength, and you believe in me when I don't believe in myself. This book will forever influence the lives of those who read it, and your support is the reason why.

To my precious children, who cheered me on and celebrated the victories throughout this process, I thank you sincerely for being my biggest advocates.

Mom and Dad, I am who I am today because of your unconditional love and support. Thank you for giving me such a precious childhood.

To my inner circle, eagle bestie friends, you made this journey fun and prioritized celebration. I drew strength from your discernment through the book writing process. Your prayers are what I believe broke through the muck to have *Nervous Breakthrough* in the world today. I deeply appreciate your encouragement and love.

To my agent, Mary, you believed in me when my platform and subscribers showed otherwise. Your heart to serve and love me as an author, not a number, is my most significant praise. Thank you for being the world's most outstanding literary agent.

To my heavenly Father, thank you for calling me to write this book. I am forever grateful for the dreaded nervous breakdown because it led me to where I am today. You have blessed me beyond measure, and I look forward to loving and serving you all the days of my life.

# Not an Autobiography

At first glance, the pages of this book may seem like an autobiography or even a memoir. Don't be fooled into believing that. The twists and turns of my struggle with severe panic and anxiety disorder didn't just pop up in 2011. They manifested over the course of a lifetime. Your fears didn't just pop up overnight either. The stories told in this book are deeply intentional. They serve a purpose: to bring realization and clarity into your own life. Through deep reflection, therapy, doctors, and most importantly, the power of God, I was able to unpack the cause and cure to become more than a conqueror over fear and anxiety. It is my intention to make that happen for you as well with this book.

You will likely find yourself woven into the fabric of my stories. I suspect there will be moments while reading when you cry out, *That's me!* There will likely be moments when you think to yourself, *I'm glad I'm not that bad.* And there may be moments when you deeply understand the heartache because you, too, have shared the same fears that wrecked you while suffering from panic and anxiety.

We are in this together. In fact, together is a great place to be. Anxiety tends to isolate. That's why what I'm about to suggest is so essential. I highly recommend that you go through this book with a small group of dear friends, or at the very least a spouse or someone you consider a mentor or leader in your life. Being in community with people you trust is the best way to achieve a breakthrough. If overcoming fear and anxiety is a priority to you, this simple step will change everything.

You may be reading this book to gain a deeper understanding of someone you deeply love who is struggling with panic and anxiety. In that case, I pray this book opens your eyes to the challenges anxiety sufferers face and that it gives you tangible resources to support them.

The back of this book includes a *Nervous Breakthrough* Study Guide to assist you. The guide consists of the Breakthrough Run Through, Scripture references, and reflection questions. Don't skip these critical sections. If you take the study guide portion of the book seriously, you will be able to identify the root cause of your fears and anxieties faster.

You deserve freedom from fear and anxiety in a world that feeds it. If you are serious about having a breakthrough, let's get started.

# CHAPTER 1

# Superwoman Tendencies

For as long as I can remember, I have strived for leading roles, top positions, highest rankings, and influence. I was only a fourth grader when our drama director asked me to step into the leading role when the star became ill days before opening night. This was a chance to shine, I thought—*I'll take it!* I stepped in and saved the day. At nine years old, I overstressed my body by pulling two all-nighters to memorize lines and blocking. After all, the show must go on. It felt invigorating to be needed, applauded, and elevated. However, I crashed and burned when the show was over; I suffered my first migraine from stress. I went to my grandparents' house to celebrate but instead had to isolate myself in a lonely room. Pounding pain pulsed through my head, and only total darkness helped alleviate it. I had never experienced a headache of that magnitude, and it scared me. Yet even the intense pain seemed a small price to pay for the accolades I received for my performance.

Peaks of success followed in high school, culminating in a campaign to become senior class president. Before I married, my last name was Pinz, so I gave out pens labeled "Pinz for President." Clever, huh? Losing was not an option for me, so I did whatever it took, and I won. Then, as if serving as president wasn't enough, I made sure to win an audition for the closing speech at graduation. I landed the opportunity and spoke to more than five thousand people.

As a fine arts major in college, my striving for the top continued. In my junior year, I basked in standing ovations every night for my performance as Catherine Sloper, the leading role in *The Heiress*. Applause became the approval my soul lived for. Where do you go when you crave the spotlight? New York City, of course! In my senior year, I traveled there to study, I pushed and shoved myself in front of talent agents, and I spoke to anyone who would listen about possible internships. Within my first month, I landed an internship and a TV commercial. Yes, that was a big deal. Wanting to match the magnitude of my successes, my boyfriend, Troy, proposed to me at Rockefeller Center in front of thousands of people. He staged a very impressive triple Salchow, which he couldn't land. When I skated to his rescue, he slid up on one knee and proposed to me in front of many onlookers. His clever maneuver gained him a firm *Yes!*

Excited to marry the love of my life, I hung up my dreams of acting and headed back to Missouri. I decided to enter the business world with a new vision: to be the best saleswoman the world has ever seen. I confidently marched into a medical equipment company to interview for a sales position—with no sales experience. They courteously declined but then offered me a customer service position instead. I accepted but fully planned to push myself into a sales role as soon as possible. Within months, I worked in sales. Within years, I led the entire sales team while studying for a master's degree in health-care administration. Needing yet another notch on my belt, I earned an MBA. Success and achievement were not just an option for me; they were my drugs of choice.

By age twenty-five, I was happily married, had started a family, and was making six figures. Though I was successful in many worldly ways, my walk with God was far from successful. I was a "CEO" Christian—Christmas and Easter only. While growing up, I learned that following God meant following a set of rules. I knew the Lord's Prayer and could even repeat it when prompted, but I never felt led to pray on my own. Why would I anyway? I didn't need God. I was doing pretty good on my own; after all, I was superwoman. I felt weak relying on anyone other than myself, so I filled my days with endless tasks, sleepless nights, and prideful conversations elevating me, myself, and I.

Our world is dripping with messages that encourage self-help, self-reliance, hustling harder, and striving longer. Memes and Pinterest boards are full of quotes like:

- *You are the master of your fate and captain of your destiny.*
- *You deserve the world, so go give it to yourself.*
- *If you believe in yourself, all things are possible.*
- *You are meant to be the hero of your own story.*

Is that really the answer? Rely on yourself, and you will be successful? What happens when you find out you are not the hero of your own story? What happens when you fail you? "Those who trust their own insight are foolish, but anyone who walks in wisdom is safe" (Prov. 28:26 NLT). Your insight lacks clarity and purpose when it's not submitted to an all-knowing God.

On a sunny Cancun beach in winter 2011, I started to fail me. While leisurely sipping on a fruity drink, an intense feeling struck me—*I need to get out of here now!* I dropped my daily-dose-of-gossip magazine and paced the pool deck. Instead of feeling better, I became short of breath, and my heart pounded. As I found it harder and harder to breathe, I excused myself from my husband Troy and our group of friends to head to my hotel room. I had no clue what was wrong. By the time I reached my room, I felt confused, disoriented, and scared.

My stomach hurt, too—pain that left me undecided if I needed to throw up or . . . well, you know. I did both. Afterward, I walked out of my room and paced the hotel floors for a bit of relief. As I made my rounds, the same question repeated in my mind: *What is wrong with me?* The maid I passed like thirty times must have wondered the same thing. As I hurried back to the room, I remembered the powerful fan I had packed and thought it might help. I placed that bad boy right up to my nose and turned it on high. As the air hit my face, it slowed my breathing enough to allow deep, cleansing breaths. Within minutes, I felt nearly normal, so I went back to the pool and told my husband what had happened. We both chalked it up to a reaction to bad water or food. After all, we were in Mexico.

## The Storm Begins Again

Several days after getting home from our trip, my right arm and leg began to tingle so severely that I found it hard to move them. I had a decent headache, and by decent, I mean painful. Suspecting a migraine, I saw my doctor. He told me to take migraine medication only if the headache disrupted my vision or became excruciating, but the headache didn't disturb me as much as the tingling on the right side of my body. Worried, I did what I absolutely do *not* recommend anyone to do—I googled my symptoms.

Listen to me carefully. Google is a dangerous tool in the hands of an anxious person. Google is not God. An Internet search can be a devil's playground, a merry-go-round that leaves you spinning with anxiety and panic. Set a boundary now to hold your fingers back from typing in your symptoms. Refuse to google alone. If you must find out more information, speak to a doctor first. Then, if you still need to know more, ask a loved one to research with you. Some practical wisdom found in the Bible says, "Plans go wrong for lack of advice; many advisors bring success" (Prov. 15:22 NLT). Don't trust just one advisor—especially one named Google. I hadn't learned this lesson yet when my Google search introduced me to a reporter who experienced a migraine on the air and had the exact same symptoms I was experiencing. Freaking out, I was sure my problem was a migraine, too, and I decided I should take the migraine medication immediately! Despite my doctor's instructions, I took the full dose.

My self-diagnosis backfired—painfully. I paced my bathroom, living room, and basement for hours with no relief, the symptoms growing worse instead of subsiding. By 6:00 a.m., the tingling felt like paralysis, and I called my primary care physician. "Go straight to the hospital," he said, mentioning I might be having a stroke.

*A stroke*, I thought. *My word!* And just like that, any shred of peace left in my body disappeared. At the ER, they whisked me away to start migraine treatment and perform a cardiac MRI to check my heart and stress levels. Everything checked out fine. *Fine? How could I be fine?*

I felt like I was dying. I asked the hospital doctor if he could give me something to calm my out-of-control body. The medication seemed like a fair request, yet I didn't quite know what I was asking for. Our hospital systems are overloaded. Staff barely have enough time to see each patient, let alone explain what's happening to our sick bodies. Traditionally, doctors treat symptoms rather than the root cause of the disease. Chapter Four discusses this in more detail, as well as how I think ignoring the root cause impacts our body, soul, and spirit. For now, I'll just tell you how I felt at that moment. The kind ER doctor did what he was trained to do, gave me Xanax, and sent me home. Just like that. No help. No explanation. No hope.

From the moment I got home, my condition grew worse. I felt completely and utterly out of my mind. Troy wondered if something had taken over my body. I couldn't relax, and nothing helped. Each time the agitation began to settle, waves of intense panic and anxiety washed over me and hit me again and again, harder and harder. I felt confused, scared, and hopeless. I'd never experienced anything like that before. My life unraveled piece by piece, and I seemed powerless to stop it. After days of suffering without relief, what I had believed for so long didn't hold power anymore. If I was the hero of my own story, why couldn't I push my way out of this chaos and pull my bootstraps up higher? I was crashing hard and fast, with no rescue in sight.

Into that crushing, crashing whirlwind, someone introduced me to a song that changed my perspective: "Praise You in the Storm," by the Casting Crowns. The chorus pierced my heart: Sometimes he calms the storm; other times he calms his child. Storms of this life *will* come. Sometimes God stops them, and sometimes he doesn't. Yet, even in the storm, we can hold on to the promise that he is with us. This was a promise I didn't understand, but I apprehensively chose to believe that God was with me. However, the thunder continued to roll, my tears continued to flow, and the beast of panic and anxiety still seemed to be in control.

## Understanding Success

What's controlling your life? My disorder was not the first thing to control me. Instead of the beast of panic and anxiety, I allowed the beast of success to rule me. How do you view success? Is it how much money you earn? Your position at work? The number of titles or influential roles you hold within your community? The list of accomplishments and awards received? I checked the box on each of these as my idea of success. I checked the online edition of the *Merriam-Webster Dictionary* for an official definition of the word *success*. It reads, "the attainment of wealth, favor, or eminence."[1] There you go; that view sounds a lot like what I believed at the time, but how does it compare to the Bible's view of success? "Observe the requirements of the LORD your God, and follow all his ways. Keep the decrees, commands, regulations, and laws written in the Law of Moses so that you will be successful in all you do and wherever you go" (1 Kings 2:3 NLT).

That is a vastly different definition. The world measures success by how much wealth, favor, influence, and power are attained. The Bible says success occurs by obeying God. One relies on self; the other depends on obedience and surrender to God. Humans are frail, mortal beings, and we lack the supernatural power and strength we need to get through life. We are shortchanged when we rely only on ourselves. Our superhero mentality only creates higher levels of stress and anxiety for us. In his book *The Anxiety Cure*, Archibald Hart says: "We were designed for camel travel, not supersonic jet behavior."[2] The world's view of success continually pushes us to run at supersonic jet speed. If we want to win the award of worldly success, there's no other way to do it except to run at fast and furious speeds. God's way to success requires the speed of a camel—slowing down, listening to, and obeying his voice. It's painfully clear that we are in a battle of opposing viewpoints, and the statistics of anxiety disorders just keep rising. It's alarming to know that 46 percent of Americans will meet the criteria for a diagnosable mental health condition sometime in their life, and half of those people develop conditions by age fourteen. Read that again! Our children may develop a diagnosable mental health illness by age fourteen. Alarming!

It's projected that 42.5 million Americans will be diagnosed with anxiety disorders each year.[3]

## Anxiety Rates Are Rising

Times are changing, and anxiety levels are soaring. Today's average high school student carries the same level of anxiety as the average psychiatric patient in the early 1950s. Anxiety is building with every decade.[4] Did you stop to process the awfulness of this observation? A psychiatric patient in the 1950s, someone hospitalized to treat their mental illness, experienced the same degree of anxiety our high school students commonly live with today! That is *not* okay!

How do we change? What do we need to learn to live more peacefully? Via Marco Polo, I recently asked my 103-year-old grandpa, who has now passed, what his secret was. Grandpa Woodrow, in my eyes, was a beacon of peace. I had never witnessed him worked up or anxious. He sat back in his wheelchair and watched my video message from his nursing home, striving to hear my voice. His demeanor told me that he was confused by this app that allowed us to talk via video, but not live. He loudly yet slowly answered my question. "Well, go to bed early, eat lots of honey, and I don't know, what else? Just take it easy. Don't worry about a lot of stuff because most of it won't happen."

As I reflected on his answer and what I knew of his life, I realized how it differed drastically from mine. It became abundantly clear to me that he traveled at a camel's pace. He participated in way fewer activities than we do today. He experienced fewer distractions, he was part of a generation with little to no screen time, and he enjoyed way more connection to family, church, and friends. All this equaled way fewer reasons to worry. Why? He didn't hear reports of every major global catastrophe, except for what his local newspaper or community shared. Every morsel of political fact or fiction didn't wait at the touch of a fingertip. He felt no need to join every activity and program available. And he certainly didn't try to prove himself to the world by continually posting on social media, as there wasn't any. Grandpa didn't run at supersonic jet speed. He lived at camel speed. (He also swore by honey as a tip to remain healthy, so stock up on honey, will ya?)

How do we know if we're leading a life defined by worldly success instead of biblical success? Check these statements against your current life:

- I rarely say no when people ask me to commit to something.
- I like praise and look for opportunities to win approval from people.
- I often compare myself to others on social media.
- I believe I am strong and can handle anything on my own.
- I don't like to ask for help.
- I rarely take vacations or schedule time for rest.
- I don't feel that it's necessary to consult God unless I'm in a crisis.
- I look for opportunities to excel and prove my worth.
- I take pride in knowing I will never let you down, even if it costs my health.
- I hold the firm belief that *If it's up to me, it will be.*
- I never like to rely on someone else to get a job done properly.

If you answered yes to even one of these statements, you have room to improve and redefine success in your life. Here is the good news: I will help you do that in the chapters to come. You will learn how to overcome fear and anxiety in a world that feeds it.

## God Replacements Instead of God Reliances

Our world feeds success in unhealthy ways. A problem arises when our strengths become God replacements instead of God "reliances," making our strength into the idol we worship instead of God. Let's stop letting the world win, and let's do things God's way. Scripture puts it like this: "Do not be conformed to this age, but be transformed by the renewing of your mind, so that you may discern what is the good, pleasing, and perfect will of God" (Rom. 12:2 CSB).

Do you want to merely conform to today's age, or would you rather experience the transforming power of renewing your mind to God's way? We don't have to live conformed to the world's ways. The New Living Translation version of Romans 12:2 says, "Don't copy the behaviors and customs of this world. . . ." Do we really want to look like everyone else? Do we want to follow the patterns of this world and be like robots who strive and are "successful" at doing the exact same things? Do you see it? The world's way creates stressed-out, anxious, depressed, but "successful" people. Renewing our minds to a higher way of thinking promises peace, slows our frantic pace, and redefines a "successful" life. The world asks us to conform to a fast-paced standard of living that promises success but creates panic. We don't have to conform to the world's way—a better way exists.

During my struggle, I learned that my superwoman tendencies and constant striving for worldly success had made me powerless to combat the beast of panic and anxiety born of the striving. Gone was my ability, influence, and strength. My superwoman cape strangled me.

## NOTES

[1] *Merriam-Webster Dictionary Online*, s.v. "success," https://www.merriam-webster.com/dictionary/success.

[2] Archibald Hart, *The Anxiety Cure: You Can Find Emotional Tranquility and Wholeness* (Nashville: Thomas Nelson, 1999), 118, Kindle.

[3] "Quick Facts and Statistics about Mental Health," Mental Health America, https://www.mhanational.org/mentalhealthfacts.

[4] Robert L. Leahy, "How Big a Problem Is Anxiety?" *Psychology Today*, April 30, 2008, https://www.psychologytoday.com/us/blog/anxiety-files/200804/how-big-problem-is-anxiety.

# CHAPTER 2

# The Label I Never Asked For

The panic remained relentless for days, but I still managed to get ready and make it to the follow-up appointment set during my hospital visit. As I paid my co-pay, I felt the panic cycle beginning—shortness of breath, tingling, and the *I need to get out of here now* compulsion. It took all I had to sit for my temperature and blood pressure readings when I just wanted to pace the hallway. The medical assistant took me back to the room to wait for the doctor. Waiting while you're anxious feels like torture. The room seemed cold, but I was sweating. After what seemed like an eternity to my panic-stricken mind, the doctor arrived. Usually, you greet your doctor with a cordial "Hello, how are you?" Not this time around. I paced the room and couldn't sit still. When Dr. Meyer entered the room, I lost it emotionally. With tears flowing and my voice trembling, I said, "What's wrong with me, Dr. Meyer? I have never felt so crazy. Something is severely wrong with me!"

He stopped to look at me, and he didn't answer right away. Instead, he thumbed through my medical records. "Christy, has something traumatic happened in your life, like a death, move, or financial hardship?" he asked.

"No, not at all," I said. "My family is great, everyone is healthy, I live in a great house, and I'm more successful than ever."

We discussed my symptoms: the racing heart, shortness of breath, inability to think straight, insomnia, headaches, and numbness in my limbs that sent me to the hospital. Dr. Meyer asked me a few questions about my job and how many hours I worked, and then he said quickly and firmly to me, "Christy, you have severe panic and anxiety disorder."

The world seemed to stop at that moment. "Excuse me, what?" I asked, mentally rejecting his words: *This can't be true! I'm always in control. Severe panic and anxiety disorder?* I'd never heard of such a thing.

"I will write you a prescription for depression," he said.

I glared at him, feeling utterly confused and panicked. "But I'm not depressed," I said, gripping my venti french vanilla latte. My answer didn't seem to change his mind, because he continued to write the prescription for depression medication.

"Since you are struggling with anxiety so badly right now, it would be wise to cut caffeine completely from your diet," he said.

As if his diagnosis were not enough, now he wanted me to sacrifice my lattes. Had this doctor gone mad? The rest of what he said about the diagnosis and medication seemed blurry. I saw his lips moving but could not comprehend his words. However, I recall his last words to me as we walked out of the exam room: "Look for physical ways to lower your stress levels. I also want you to dig deep and find out how you have gotten yourself into this situation. Last, look into a counselor and support of the church." With those final thoughts to ponder from my wise primary care doctor, I began my journey toward understanding fear and anxiety.

## Understanding Panic and Anxiety Disorder

Understanding anxiety may not be a top priority for you at this moment, but please hang in there with me. Having a general understanding of anxiety can not only help you but also give you tools and wisdom when dealing with someone else who is suffering from anxiety. The facts don't lie; our world is dripping with people suffering from intense fears and anxieties. Education on the matter can help you be a better human being. Take a crash course with me real quick.

What exactly is panic and anxiety disorder? First, we must understand that not all anxiety is the same. There are many types of anxiety disorders. You may have heard of generalized anxiety, obsessive-compulsive disorder, post-traumatic stress disorder, and social anxiety. The cause and symptoms of each of these types of anxiety often look different for everyone. My disorder was severe panic *and* anxiety, which caused sudden panic attacks that left me feeling terrified when no real danger appeared present. It was common for me to feel completely out of control. It's important to note that not all panic attacks are created equal. Below is a list of all the symptoms I have felt during a panic attack. In my research, I found that these symptoms have appeared in other people as well. In milder spells, I would only experience a few of these symptoms. In more aggressive attacks that would come and go for weeks, I could experience all of them:

- Fast or irregular heartbeat
- Chest tightness and heaviness (a load of bricks on your chest)

- Upset stomach and nausea
- Diarrhea
- Shortness of breath
- Weakness or dizziness
- Feeling hot or cold
- Tingly or numb limbs, especially in arms and hands
- Hives or itchy spots on the skin
- Hair loss
- Tension headaches
- Clenched or sore jaw
- Severe insomnia
- Racing, uncontrollable thoughts
- Thoughts of ending one's life

Medical professionals say panic attacks don't last long. That's true, but each one leaves a permanent imprint on your soul, especially if you're enduring what seems like a never-ending cycle. Would my cycle become a life sentence? Add fear to that list of panic-related effects.

I have always thought of myself as reliable, successful, a problem solver, intelligent, and confident, so at first I resisted the label of severe panic and anxiety disorder, and I even refused to start the medication. After all, I exemplified the girl who always had it together—the overachiever, the leader, the person who never needs help and is always helping others. *How in the world did this happen to me?* I wondered over and over.

Something didn't compute. I've always prided myself on having a quick wit, but now I wrestled with constant fear. My sound mind crumpled beneath an avalanche of panic and anxiety. Nothing made any sense, but I knew one thing for sure—I needed change in my life. I just didn't know how to start.

## Panic Forced Me to Stop

The tingling, shortness of breath, and heart pounding would not let up, but I got up and dressed for my job anyway. Work had piled up over our vacation, and I needed to take care of it. The commute didn't go well, because I couldn't clear my mind to focus on driving. How in the world would I string together intelligent sales pitches to land business for my company when I could barely drive? I realized I needed time off, but I prided myself on rarely resting or taking sick days. Just craving a break indicated that something must be deeply wrong with me. I needed to discuss what was happening with my boss, but could I even get the words out? My panic forced me to stop at three gas stations to throw up, but somehow, I managed to pull myself together to finish the drive and find my boss. I walked into his office feeling flustered, weak, and full of emotion.

"Steve, I am not physically and emotionally healthy right now, and I need to take a leave of absence," I said, tears streaming down my face. His faced showed major concern. He wasn't used to seeing a weak and out-of-control Christy.

He kept it short and sweet. "Go get better," he said. "Don't worry about work!"

I walked out of his office. I was not sure if I would ever return.

I know what some of you are thinking: *It would be nice if I could take a break, too.* I realize you may not have an understanding boss or team. You may have obligations at home and not have built-in help. I know my boss blessed me with support when I needed it most, but we'll explore your avenues of support in Chapter Eight, "The Company You Keep."

Even though my boss understood, sharing my weakness with him felt incredibly hard. If you haven't guessed by now, I consumed myself with my job. I never stopped working; I was the very definition of a workaholic. Admitting I needed help was not typical of me, but here's the thing about panic and anxiety—it will make you vulnerable whether you like it or not. If you hide your weaknesses instead of opening up about them, your panic and anxiety will consume you.

My drive home from work proved more difficult than getting there, and I didn't think it could get much worse. I must have stopped at five or six gas stations, plus a Hardee's, in a thirty-mile stretch. The fast-food workers must have thought I was crazy, as I walked in and out almost twenty times. Yet, I felt too anxious to leave the side of the toilet. I even contemplated calling 911. I didn't understand at the time, but panic and anxiety mess with your entire body. It's just as much physical as mental. Upon arriving home, it suddenly struck me that I had never stopped to pray despite my fear, panic, stress, and anxiety. I had become so used to relying on myself that prayer didn't seem feasible.

Our world has a problem, as its collective mindset is to fix our own problems and depend on ourselves to meet our needs. That's self-help. But the truth is, self-help is no help at all. What do you do when your "self" fails you? As I faced that exact situation, I pondered, *Where does my help come from if it doesn't come from me?*

## Childhood Prayers

While my parents are wonderful people, we did not pray for help in our family. I learned to memorize and recite prayers as a child, but those prayers never meant anything to me. Those prayers seemed only to be powerless, repetitious, religious words. I prayed out of tradition, not out of love for Jesus. The first time I really prayed after my panic episodes began, I sounded half-hearted at best, but it was a start, a small glimpse of what it means to call on God for help. Scripture is overflowing with encouragement, but I had no idea. "I lift up my eyes to the mountains—where does my help come from? My help comes from the LORD, the Maker of heaven and earth" (Ps. 121:1–2 NIV).

There aren't many places to look except up when you're down. I looked up to the Maker of heaven and earth, God himself, the only One who could provide help and peace. Self-reliance failed me, so I tried surrender of self. I surrendered to a God who loves me and desires to free me of my fears and anxiety.

My friend gave me a small brown cross that hung on the wall in my bedroom. The cross says, "Believe all things are possible." Embedded in my Catholic roots, I recall kneeling to pray to a large cross in front of the church. I was desperate, so I decided to try a kneeling prayer to that cross. With tears streaming down my face, I cried out, "God, I don't know why I'm going through this, but you do. Please help me. I surrender. My life is yours. I give up. Please take over."

After I prayed, the only thing I knew to do next was read and gain knowledge about anxiety. Between waves of panic, I devoured as many books as I could get my hands on, hoping they would shed some light on my situation. Within a few days, I finished *Fearless* by Max Lucado, *The Anxiety Cure* by Archibald Hart, and *Battlefield of the Mind* by Joyce Meyer.

As the seriousness of my disorder took hold, my family and friends began to pray, too. I needed their help, so my mother took care of our two little boys while Troy tried to focus on his job. I had to lock myself in my room, in complete isolation, due to the severity of my anxiety and panic episodes. I truly felt out of my mind and body. Everything I once thought I was good at became inconceivable to me. All the success I gained and achievements I earned became powerless in the face of severe panic and anxiety. I no longer controlled any aspect of my life. I couldn't even pull myself together enough to step out of my bedroom to watch my son's first steps. Missing that moment filled me with guilt and still haunts me to this day.

On my bedroom floor, feeling scared and alone, I learned that the world's view of success had conformed me entirely. The world's ways contributed to my rising stress levels and praised my bad habits; they turned me into a workaholic, money-watching, achievement-driven, prideful wife and mother. This breakdown came without my approval. When trials come without your permission—believe me, they always come without your permission—it changes you. Mine challenged me in ways I never thought possible and caused me to think differently. I started having big thoughts like, *Are the world's ways God's ways?* In a crisis, you begin to take inventory of what's important. Suddenly, the notches on my belt of success seemed meaningless. I came across this great verse in Isaiah 55:8–9: "'For my thoughts are not your thoughts, neither are your ways my ways,' declares the LORD. 'As the heavens are higher than the earth, so are my ways higher than your ways, and my thoughts than your thoughts'" (NIV).

## Shift Our Focus Higher

I knew heaven was higher than the earth, but I didn't live like it. How often are we all guilty of living life with an earthly viewpoint instead of a heavenly one? How do we shift our focus higher, to God's way?

In Matthew 16, Jesus predicted his death to his disciples. He told them he would die horribly but would rise again on the third day. Well, that didn't sit well with his buddy Peter. He told Jesus not to talk that way. He wasn't going to die. Jesus's response to Peter is mind-boggling and is perhaps the answer we all need to reflect on living life from God's perspective instead of the world's. "Jesus turned to Peter and said, 'Get away from me, Satan! You are a dangerous trap to me. You are seeing things merely from a human point of view, not from God's'" (Matt. 16:23 NLT).

Jesus saw heaven's viewpoint, and Peter saw an earthly view, which Jesus rebuked. So much fear and anxiety come from our worldly, human ideas. What if we stop to ask questions from a godly viewpoint?

- *God, what are you doing here?*
- *How can I grow and learn from this?*
- *Where are you, God, in this?*
- *How can I consider this trial a joy?*

Sadly, most of us dismiss a trial and only count it as a loss, entirely missing out on heaven's viewpoint. Since his ways *are* higher, we must look at our situations and circumstances from God's higher viewpoint rather than our limited human one.

My storm of panic and anxiety still raged with no end in sight. However, something shifted inside me. I became keenly aware that a higher way of living existed. Could God's way offer a solution to my mess?

## Physical and Spiritual Forces at Work

My nights strung long and dark, and my days boasted more downs than ups. I experienced another batch of severe panic attacks about seven days into this mess. I hadn't eaten for days, and sleep seemed like something I would never do again. I lost weight rapidly, and my hair came out in clumps in the shower. My mental state deteriorated, too, and in that dark frame of mind, my eyes locked in on the hunting guns in the corner of our room. Although the guns were unloaded, I knew where the bullets were kept.

*Why don't you just use those guns?* whispered a voice in my head that sounded like darkness. *You're never going to get through this. This torture will be your life forever—you might as well end it now*. I considered whether death might be easier than the hellish torment I faced.

"No!" I cried, falling to the floor sobbing. "That is not true! I could never do something like that!" I covered the guns with blankets to hide the visual reminder of the temptation set before me by the kingdom of darkness to end my life.

I never dreamed my life would get so dark. I became part of the statistics of suicidal ideations. In 2019, according to the National Institute of Mental Health, twelve million people age eighteen or older reported having serious thoughts of suicide. I became one of the twelve million, and it was severe, dark, and real.

Read the following carefully if you're thinking about ending your life and perhaps have already created a plan. I understand. I see your pain. I know you're not selfish and that you just want freedom from pain and torment. I realize you may believe the lie that it will be better if you're gone. The lie whispers that you're a burden to your family and friends—it insists they'll be better off without you. Those are lies I momentarily believed, too. But I promise, not one ounce of those lies is the truth. No one can guarantee a life without pain and suffering. No one is exempt. We are, however, guaranteed to be more than conquerors through Christ if we choose his path. A life filled with God's grace and love can get us through anything we face, including the darkness of suicidal thoughts. Choosing that path of overcoming is not easy. Immediately after I became aware of my dark thoughts, I told someone I trusted. If you don't have someone you trust, call the National Suicide Prevention Lifeline at 988. When you bring these thoughts into the light, they lose the power they held when they hid in the darkness.

When Troy came home from work that day, I collapsed into his arms, screaming, "Honey, my day was so hard—it was so hard!" Holding me, he glanced toward the corner of our room.

"Why are my hunting guns covered up?" he asked. I told him about the dark thoughts and how the guns tempted me to consider them an option. Holding me tighter, he said, "We'll get through this together."

## Fighting for My Life

While researching anxiety and depression, I hadn't taken the prescribed medication yet. Have you read the side effects of some antidepressants? It's enough to give an average person a panic attack. Can you imagine the fear it raised in an already panicked person like me? Between dark temptations, obsessive thoughts about medication, and panic attacks, I shouldn't have been surprised when my anxiety grew worse as the evening rolled around. Having consecutive panic attacks felt like running continuous marathons. Once one race concluded, I had to sprint to another. As dramatic as it sounds, it was worse. I felt like I was fighting for my life.

As Troy and I grew sick and tired of this painful pattern, I saw a side of him I had never seen before. He covered me with his strong arms that evening and boldly prayed this prayer:

> God, I take authority over this situation. We rebuke
> what is happening to Christy right now and do not
> accept it. We ask for wisdom as soon as possible so
> we can begin to understand what is happening to her.
> Please allow her to rest this evening and for her body to
> calm. In your name, we pray, amen!

A prayer with a bold proclamation! "We . . . do not accept it. We ask for wisdom." Did you know God answers our prayers? Maybe not in a way we expect, but he does answer. It's imperative to remember, "God is our refuge and strength, a very present help in trouble"

(Ps. 46:1 KJV). Do you see that? "God is" help in trouble, not "you" are the help in trouble.

Despite anxiety's interruptions, I slept for the first time in days after Troy prayed. When a wave of fear hit me, I let it throw me into God's arms. I stayed connected to him all night, and I prayed out loud every time waves rolled in. I discovered a new wave rolling in, too—a wave of hope loomed.

# CHAPTER 3

# Not Me—I'm Always in Control

I believe control is an illusion that leads you down a dead-end street. My dead end started when my primary care physician looked at me and said, "Christy, you have severe panic and anxiety disorder." Nothing stops you faster than a diagnosis that slows you down. With anxiety disorders on the rise, many are experiencing these slowdowns. Regularly, the world tells us to believe we can control our destiny, manifest success, create opportunities, and control our circumstances. Those big ideas contain some truth, along with some significant lies. The lies packed into these truths are poisonous, and even if the truths outweigh the lies, just a little bit of poison can still kill you.

## The Danger of Self-Help

Self-help teachers preach flashy statements like, "You are meant to be the hero of your own story." I'm not going to lie; being the hero of my own story sounds captivating, and I want it by default. I love to be in control, and I think I'm pretty good at it. Being the hero of my story leads me to believe that I am in control, that I can "make s\*\*t happen."

Another common phrase in the world of self-help influencers that promotes the illusion of control is, "Live your truth." Candidly, I don't understand how you can live *your* truth. For example, if my truth is the stoplight is red and means to go, and your truth is the stoplight is green and means go, then living my truth creates a huge problem! Someone must be right. A truth that contradicts itself is no longer valid. I have concluded that living your truth is a dangerous lie, a lie that teaches that no ultimate truth exists. Because you are the hero of your own story, you live your truth, I'll live mine, and we will all be anxious, depressed, and confused together. My point is that something must be true to be factual. I can't live a truth separate from someone else's truth while both of us are "right."

What is the ultimate truth? An excerpt from a *Focus on the Family* article beautifully explains the idea of ultimate truth:

> If we have ultimate truth, it gives us both a way to explain the world around us and a basis for making decisions. Without it, we're alone. We're just 6 billion organisms running around, bumping into each other with nothing unifying to work for or believe in. It's every man for himself. And we're without a purpose; if there's no true story of where we came from and why we're here, then there's nothing that really gives our lives meaning. Sounds a little depressing, huh? And maybe frightening.[1]

That is frightening! I lived a life of control, and I bumped into everything that threatened my control. Living that way is hopeless.

I believe that the ultimate source of truth is the Word of God, the Bible. God's Word is right, good, authentic, genuine, and true. John 8:32 declares that the Word is truth and that walking in the truth will set you free. Perhaps you have innocently said, "I'm the hero of my story" or "Go live your truth" while celebrating the power you feel by believing and stating those phrases. I would like to ask you, with no judgment, a few honest and straightforward questions. How does it feel to be the hero of your own story? Is living your truth really a path to freedom?

With the journey I have endured, I sincerely believe in the truth. We are not the heroes of our stories; Jesus is. He is the ultimate source of truth. I have lived the life of thinking I'm the hero. Plus, I tried the *there is no truth, live your truth* approach, and it got me nowhere but a nervous breakdown. The truth found in John 14:6 says, "[Jesus is] the way, the truth, and the life" (NLT). Many self-help books, even those referred to as Christian, present lies as truths that contradict the Bible. For example, Proverbs 28:26 is crystal clear on self-help: "Those who trust in themselves are fools, but those who walk in wisdom are kept safe" (NIV). I honestly don't care how this book is labeled for sale; I wanted to mark it self-help to get you to read it. Let's be honest: a "surrendered-life-to-Jesus-help" isn't as popular as self-help. In fact, there isn't even a sale category for it. The point is: self-help is no help at all.

I don't believe the authors of self-help books are intentionally misleading you. They want to empower and love their readers well. But that's the problem with lies. They often sound good and are believable but are packed with poison. I believed a poisonous lie similar to the self-help web of lies, and it goes like this: *I am always in control.* I thought my superwoman control tendencies were sexy and alluring. I had mastered the ability to influence people's decisions and behaviors and felt responsible for doing so. I often confidently predicted how an event would come to be. I ruled my life and those around me like a queen, kicking butt and taking names, as the saying goes.

There is a big difference between healthy planning and the disorder of manifesting control in your life. Planning is biblical. In fact, a popular verse that gets quoted regarding planning is, "In their hearts humans plan their course, but the LORD establishes their steps" (Prov. 16:9 NIV). There is nothing wrong with a good solid plan, but do you hold that plan loosely? Are you willing to lay that plan down if the Lord leads you in a new direction? The world so influences our lives that it is rare to study or practice living a life submitted to God. Making my own plans led to destructive and alarming results. I controlled my circumstances to help manage the deep fears and anxieties I had inside. Control is exhausting, and it comes with a high price.

## The Need to Control

According to WebMD, "People with anxiety disorders feel a need to control everything around them in order to feel at peace." The writer of this article indicates that control and anxiety disorders go hand in hand. Let's do some digging to make sense of what WebMD is trying to teach us. What is at the root of control? When I control, I'm trying to protect my peace. How does one "feel" at peace? By taking control. I liked to control things by dominating every situation. It's evident by the diagnosis I received that peace did not result from that control. What are your controlling ways?

- Do you always have to be right?
- Do you try to determine outcomes in advance to move things in your favor?
- Do you rarely take the blame?
- Do you like being the center of attention?
- Do you rarely seek advice from others?

- Do you like the way you do things best and therefore seldom rely on others for help?
- Do you like to micromanage people?
- Do you constantly check your bank statements and stock performances?
- Do you speak white lies from time to time to make your situation look better?

Is something else coming to your mind that you do to take control of a situation? Let's stop right here. Part of overcoming a problem is acknowledging a problem. Circle the above statements that properly reflect how you like to remain in control. In the margin spaces of this section, add anything not mentioned. I understand that, if you are a control sufferer, writing in a clean book may not be an option for you, so this is your cue to grab a clean sheet of paper or a journal to do this exercise. I'm proud of you for taking the time to process your controlling ways.

Now it's time to evaluate. Does the outcome of those statements you just identified bring peace? Hopefully, I have gotten your thoughts flowing, and you are processing the question, *What is peace?* To answer that clearly, I think we must define or perhaps redefine peace. Is peace a feeling or a state of being? For example, can you feel peace when the circumstances around you are crumbling? "Absolutely not" is how I would have answered that question pre-nervous breakdown. I assumed that peace is something you achieve, something that manifests when you follow all the proper steps and manage yourself in a way that is free of disturbances.

The world seems to preach that peace is possible when no fear or violence is present. Interestingly, there is no shortage of fear and violence among us. The increasing number of conflicts and amount of hatred toward one another and rising fear and anxiety disorders don't seem to highlight a peaceful world. This leads me to the question at hand: Can peace be achieved by checking all the right boxes and doing the right yoga moves? Is it possible to enter a state of tranquility or zen managed by you? Do we have the power to cultivate peace from within? What if the world has got it wrong, and peace is a person?

What if the solution to control is surrender, and surrender leads to peace? The world teaches us to never wave the white flag. *Always keep going. Don't you dare show weakness. Keep on keeping on. Hustle harder.* The world offers no accolades to surrender; it frowns on it. Surrender paints signs of weakness. What if surrender is a strength? Please follow me closely: I'm not proposing surrendering to the world, but I'm asking you to ponder what it would look like to surrender to Jesus, the person who is the Prince of Peace. What if peace is a state of being that starts with surrendering to the Prince of Peace? We will dive into this in much more detail in Chapter Ten.

## Fan, Not Follower

2007 was a pivotal year in my walk with Jesus. I had been married for about three years and had no kids. We had some passion starting for becoming more than CEO Christians (Christmas and Easter only), so we decided to go to church one morning. In my heart, I knew I had sinned against God and wanted to get back on track with him. At the end of the service, I heard the pastor say that you can do it now if you want to give your life to Jesus. He asked us to raise our hands and repeat after him, repeat something about confessing with our mouths and believing in our hearts that Jesus is Lord. Just like that, I repeated what is known as the salvation prayer.

I felt the heat of embarrassment rise through my body as I raised my hand to accept Jesus. Exactly why did I feel embarrassed? The pastor told the rest of the room to close their eyes and bow their heads, so nobody saw me make this commitment, including my husband. So why did I feel that way? Perhaps my embarrassment came from shame. God and I were not exactly besties, and I knew he wasn't a priority in my life. I had good intentions—I wanted him to be a priority, but unfortunately, I didn't know how. I needed accountability, yet no one held me accountable for the decision I had just made to follow Jesus, including myself. I walked out of that church service and went back to my same habits, same thought patterns, and same problems. Not surrendering to God, I chose to be in charge of myself and proud of it. I popped into church whenever I felt like it. I never opened my Bible and did not pray. No fruit came from that prayer I repeated in church.

Then 2011 hit. The storm of severe panic and anxiety disorder came rolling through. Remember the tearful prayer I prayed? *God, I don't know why I'm going through this, but you do. Please help me. I surrender. My life is yours. I give up. Please take over.* After a successful night of sleep, surrender from the previous day, and prayers from my husband and family, something unusual happened. In my bathroom, I heard a still, small voice tell me to reach out to a friend from college whom I had not talked to in over seven years. The prompting felt peaceful, out of the blue, almost audible, and it directed me clearly. I know what you may be thinking: *She heard a voice in her head while standing in the bathroom. She really is crazy!* Listen, I feel you; it seemed crazy to me as well. I realize I'm at risk of you shutting this book completely, but please understand that it was not a regular occurrence for me to hear this type of direction. However, I knew with certainty it was God.

I didn't realize it at the time, but in the book of John, Jesus said his sheep listen to his voice (John 10:27). I heard, and I listened to the still, small voice and reached out to my old college friend. It turned out she had gone through an identical diagnosis. Was it a coincidence that I reached out to her? I highly doubt it. Think about this for a moment: What is the probability of being prompted to reach out to someone from seven years ago who strangely went through an identical situation? If I were wise enough to figure out mathematical probabilities, I would figure it out for you. I would venture to guess the likelihood of this just being a coincidence would be highly unlikely.

In my opinion, God orchestrated the prompting to contact my old friend, who poured wisdom into me to help me get healthy. She told me I wouldn't make it through panic and anxiety disorder without a relationship with Jesus. Then she gave me lots of godly resources for studying anxiety and depression. She encouraged me to seek Christian counseling, and she encouraged me to listen to my primary care physician and trust his course of action with the medication he had prescribed for me. Her call confirmed what I already knew and became an answer to Troy's prayer: "We ask for wisdom as soon as possible so we can begin to understand what is happening to her." My husband's prayer and my willingness to take a chance on the call to my friend turned the tide in my favor. The answer became crystal clear. I needed to surrender to Jesus, lay down pride and pick up humility, and untie my superwoman cape and drop it at the feet of Jesus. I needed to make him my first response, not my last resort.

## Nervous Breakthrough

In 2007, I considered Jesus my last resort, not a top priority in my life. I recently asked him about my salvation when I repeated that prayer in church, and I heard him whisper, *Your heart didn't understand what your lips were saying.* According to Romans 10:9, I was saved by the grace of God in 2007 because I believed in my heart and confessed with my mouth that Jesus is Lord. Yet, that moment of salvation wasn't the end of the story, it was only the beginning. Jesus knew how my journey would go, that I wouldn't truly surrender my life to him until 2011, when I had my nervous breakdown. I was only a fan of Jesus during that time of my life. Fans will cheer for you when you are doing something great, but fans will often turn their back on you when the going gets rough. I liked Jesus enough to celebrate the good things he did, like being born of a virgin so I could celebrate Christmas with piles of gifts under the tree, and rising from the dead so I could hand out yummy Cadbury Creme Eggs at Easter, but I wasn't interested in changing my life to follow him. Following Jesus would have meant commitment and intentionality in reading the Bible, attending church, and praying.

I didn't see a need for all that because I was doing pretty well for myself without the "follower" stuff. Fans will often turn into followers when they realize their fandom doesn't buy anything but fear. That's how it happened for me. After being consumed with fear, I became more than just a fan; I became a faithful follower of Jesus while facing a nervous breakdown. My breakdown moment became the springboard for my life's mission and calling. I redefined that moment not as a nervous breakdown but as a nervous breakthrough, hence the title of this book. I finally looked up while crying on my bedroom floor, desperate for help, inundated with fear, and experiencing a breakdown.

As I write this chapter, the biggest cry of my heart is for you to understand a critical point I learned the hard way. Salvation is not surrendering. It's a step in the right direction, but it's not the final act of obedience. Salvation is a decision. Surrender is a commitment. I mentioned that we will explore in detail, in Chapter Ten, how to know if you are living a life surrendered to Jesus, but for now, I want to give you the opportunity to accept and receive salvation.

## It's More than Santa and the Easter Bunny

Salvation comes from Jesus. We must accept and receive his saving grace to be saved from sin and death. Knowledge of Jesus is not the same as accepting and receiving him. We must learn to believe by faith and receive Jesus as Lord of our lives. When we do this, it changes the way we live and speak. Jesus's story is so much more than Christmas and Easter, Santa and the Easter Bunny. Sadly, our world has minimized the life of Jesus to commercialized events and holidays. The story of Jesus is deep, impactful, and life changing. The truth is that it should challenge you. You should feel the tension of its mystery and wonder.

Over two thousand years ago, God sent his one and only son to this earth. He was born of a virgin named Mary (Jesus's birth is what we celebrate on Christmas). He grew up and lived a sinless life. He died a brutal death, and his blood was poured out for our sins on the cross as a sacrifice. His blood canceled the debt of sin. He paid the price for us on the cross so we could be forgiven and have eternal life. Upon his death, the veil tore, and we were made right with God. His death didn't end in death; on the third day, he rose again (that's when we celebrate Easter). Fun fact: Did you know that Christianity is the only religion that follows a risen God? How extraordinary!

After Jesus rose again, he showed himself to over five hundred people, did life with them for forty days, and then ascended into heaven to be seated at the right hand of God. After his ascension into heaven, the Holy Spirit poured out onto those who believed in him, and the church of Jesus's followers, not fans, began to spread rapidly. That same power of the Holy Spirit is available to you, for those who receive and believe Jesus as the way, the truth, and the life. Our eternal destination is sealed to an eternity in heaven as soon as we receive and believe. Christ adopts us into his heavenly family.

Do you want to receive and believe? Have you identified that you are just a fan and want to become a true follower? The first step is to understand the gift of salvation. Have you ever been given a wonderful gift at Christmas that you never bothered to use because you didn't take time to read the directions? One time, my kids received a robot, the most popular toy of the year, as a gift. It picked up objects on command, told jokes, challenged you with critical thinking ideas, and even synced with other robots to perform more exciting features. But guess what? It never made it out of the box. Why? Because nobody in our family took the time to understand it and read the directions to use it to its full potential. Similarly, we often don't take the time to understand the gift of salvation by reading God's Word, the instruction manual; we totally miss out.

Next, we must believe. In one of the most famous scriptures of all time we learn, "For God so loved the world that he gave his one and only Son, that whoever believes in him shall not perish but have eternal life" (John 3:16 NIV). To receive eternal life, we must believe in Jesus. Believing is different than knowing. You can know the story of Jesus but not believe in it. It takes faith to believe that Jesus was born of a virgin, died, and rose from the dead. I get it. It's a remarkable story. Yet believing is accepting the claims of Jesus as truth, not just as a fable or good story. Do you believe it? Then receive him today. Salvation is a generous gift from a loving Father.

> *Father, today I accept you as my personal Lord and Savior. I am sorry for my sins, and I thank you for your sacrifice on the cross for me. Help me be more than just a fan; I want to follow you. In Jesus's name, amen.*

Welcome to the family of God. The journey of increasing your faith and reducing your fears awaits you in the chapters to come.

## NOTE

[1]Lindy Keffer, "Absolute Truth in a RelativisticWorld," Focus on the Family, April 1, 2019, https://www.focusonthefamily.com/church/absolute-truth/.

# CHAPTER 4

# Fear the Bigger Pandemic

Being discharged from the hospital should have made me feel better. After all, I had somewhat of a diagnosis now: panic and anxiety disorder. The solution seemed to be a drug designed to calm my out-of-control body and follow-up with my primary care physician for more treatment options. There is a standard of care in the United States that assumes releasing someone from the hospital means they should be in a stable condition. It's easy to measure stability when it's physical because the medical professionals have vital signs and pain measurements, but how about when it's mental? I was never asked, "How is your thought life?" I was asked, "Do you want to harm yourself?" At that moment, I didn't, and I believe I would have been honest about the first question if someone had dared ask me.

"Horrible!" I would have replied. "I'm scared, I can't focus, and frankly, I have no idea how to stop the scary thoughts that are relentlessly taking me under. I feel like I'm drowning with no end in sight."

Our hospital systems are pretty good at identifying the physical symptoms we experience and prescribing medications to fix them, but they fail to recognize that our thoughts also lead to physical symptoms. Could there be a correlation between mental, physical, and spiritual wellness that a balanced approach could measure? What if we began to treat the entire person instead of just the physical body?

## Treating the Holistic Person

In Caroline Leaf's book *Cleaning Up Your Mental Mess*, she says, "We can go three weeks without food, three days without water, three minutes without oxygen—but we can't even go for three seconds without thinking."[1] With the thought avalanche engulfing me, I was being buried alive with no escape. Yet, I made no connection between my thoughts and my physical symptoms, and neither did the health-care professionals. I interpret Leaf's words as: your thoughts matter. If we can't go three seconds without thinking, then we think many thoughts per day. Can negative thoughts hurt your body? Do positive thoughts contribute to a healthier you?

Leaf continues with a mind-staggering fact:

> When our thinking is toxic, it can mess up the stress response, which then starts working against us instead of for us. This, in turn, can make us more vulnerable to disease, which is why many researchers now believe that toxic stress is responsible for up to approximately 90 percent of illness, including heart disease, cancer, and diabetes. Only 5–10 percent of disease is said to come from genetic factors alone.[2]

If only 5–10 percent of diseases come from genetic factors, how much disease comes from toxic stress that derives from striving, hustling, trying to prove your worth, feeling bitter, and being unable to forgive?

Can you imagine an intake form that not only asks about physical symptoms but also about your mental and spiritual well-being? In the next chapter, we will cover what I call smoke alarms. I believe if we were more diligent about smoke alarms, we wouldn't get to the point of hospitalization as often. At any rate, these questions would ask you about your work–home–life balance, nutrition, sleep hygiene, friendships, marriage, parenting, faith, and finances. Then you would dig deeply to evaluate if you are unwilling to forgive anyone. It would end by asking you to take inventory of your negative thoughts. Once completed, a doctor, a mental health professional, and a spiritually wise Christian leader would review the information and work together to treat your illness.

Unfortunately, our health-care system does not work this way. Separating our physical, spiritual, and mental health is *not* working. If it were, would anxiety and depression be at all-time highs? Would the suicide rates be climbing? The facts don't lie. "Nearly 800,000 people die by suicide in the world each year, which is roughly one death every 40 seconds. Suicide is the 2nd leading cause of death in the world for those aged 15–24 years. Depression is the leading cause of disability worldwide."[3] You can't read alarming statics of that nature and wonder how we got here. Looking at the pandemic of fear, anxiety, toxic stress, and depression differently is the only way out of this mess. Keeping church for Sunday mornings, doctors for offices and hospitals, and psychiatrists and psychologists for comfy couches is only doing a major disservice to our lives.

## Made of Three

God's Word tells us we are spirit, soul, and body. The Bible's authority on trichotomy is undoubtedly sufficient. G. H. Pember describes trichotomy as follows:

> Now the body we may term the sense-consciousness, the soul the self-consciousness, and the spirit the God-consciousness. For the body gives us the five senses; the soul comprises the intellect which aids us in the present state of existence, and the emotions which proceed from the senses; while the spirit is our noblest part, which came directly from God, and by which alone we are able to apprehend and worship Him.[4]

The world pays great attention to our senses, to what we can see and feel. I don't think anyone would disagree that, in the United States, preserving our physical body is the gold standard of living. Undergoing plastic surgery procedures to smooth out wrinkles, tuck in the neck flap, and cut off some flab is just the norm. Why? Because we put a great deal of importance on our physical bodies, what we can see and feel. Focusing on your body is not wrong, but it's not balanced to just care about the body alone. When we focus on one part over the others, we become unbalanced. Imagine a tricycle; let's say that only the back wheel got pumped up. Would the tricycle work if only one tire had air in it? Body, soul, and spirit need equal parts of "air" to function correctly.

## Don't Just Blame the Doctors

I propose a dream of a health-care system that seems far-fetched and highly unlikely, a system in which doctors, mental health professionals, and church leaders come together as a team to treat a person in three parts. The truth is that we don't just have a long way to go with the medical community; we also have a long way to go with the church. As a result of the work I do with fear and anxiety, I have come across many men and women who have been abused by their church after admitting to having mental health issues. Upon confessing their struggle, their leaders shamed them into believing their faith wasn't strong enough. They heard abusive comments like, "If you had more faith, you wouldn't be struggling." This abusive behavior does not occur in all churches, but it happens in more churches than we would like to admit. My friend Chris Morris advocates for mental health awareness, especially in the church. In his book *Whispers in the Pews*, Chris collected a series of essays that bring to light real-life stories of people who have endured spiritual abuse. One anonymous piece recounts abuse from the pulpit; here is an excerpt:

> I am a whole person—soul, mind, and body. And I am a follower of Jesus Christ. But after a forty-five-minute sermon at my church last winter, I felt like a very poor representation of personhood and of Christ. The pastor had spoken on the topic of anxiety that morning. He had some solid points about the value of training our minds to focus on things other than worst-case scenarios, even bringing up Cognitive Behavioral Therapy, which I've often used. But I had some challenges with what he shared from the pulpit too. He also said there was no need for medication in the life of a Christian. He urged those of us who use medications to reevaluate, to quit concentrating on our anxiety in favor of inviting Jesus into our anxiety so He could heal it. When I left church that morning, I felt less-than. Lazy. Faithless. I felt as though I'd failed.[5]

As someone who took a cocktail of three different anxiety meds and antidepressants to cope with severe panic and anxiety disorder,

I shudder at sitting through a sermon in which the pastor says, "There is no need for medication in the life of a Christian." In the same breath, I also shudder at doctors prescribing antidepressants and Xanax like it's candy. What gives? Where is the healthy balance between faith and medication?

Let's start with faith. I believe it is impossible to overcome anxiety without building your faith. The Bible is a prescription that cannot be overdosed. The Bible contains hundreds of passages that urge us not to walk in fear. The spirit of fear is not from God. Peace is from God, and we walk in the peace of God by knowing the Word of God. To help you build your faith muscles, I'm going to list my top ten favorite passages on not being afraid. Bookmark this page, and memorize these scriptures. Meditating on what God says about fear will bring peace to your life.

- "For God hath not given us the spirit of fear; but of power, and of love, and of a sound mind." (2 Tim. 1:7 KJV)
- "There is no fear in love. But perfect love drives out fear, because fear has to do with punishment. The one who fears is not made perfect in love." (1 John 4:18 NIV)
- "So do not fear, for I am with you; do not be dismayed, for I am your God. I will strengthen you and help you; I will uphold you with my righteous right hand." (Isa. 41:10 NIV)
- "Even when I walk through the darkest valley, I will not be afraid, for you are close beside me. Your rod and your staff protect and comfort me." (Ps. 23:4 NLT)
- "So be strong and courageous! Do not be afraid and do not panic before them. For the LORD your God will personally go ahead of you. He will neither fail you nor abandon you." (Deut. 31:6 NLT)

- "Suddenly, a fierce storm struck the lake, with waves breaking into the boat. But Jesus was sleeping. The disciples went and woke him up, shouting, 'Lord, save us! We're going to drown!' Jesus responded, 'Why are you afraid? You have so little faith!' Then he got up and rebuked the wind and waves, and suddenly there was a great calm." (Matt. 8:24–26 NLT)
- "God is within her, she will not fall; God will help her at break of day." (Ps. 46:5 NIV)
- "They will have no fear of bad news; their hearts are steadfast, trusting in the LORD." (Ps. 112:7 NIV)
- "God is our refuge and strength, an ever-present help in trouble. Therefore we will not fear, though the earth give way and the mountains fall into the heart of the sea, though its waters roar and foam and the mountains quake with their surging." (Ps. 46:1–3 NIV)
- "Those who live in the shelter of the Most High will find rest in the shadow of the Almighty. This I declare about the LORD: He alone is my refuge, my place of safety; he is my God, and I trust him. For he will rescue you from every trap and protect you from deadly disease. He will cover you with his feathers. He will shelter you with his wings. His faithful promises are your armor and protection. Do not be afraid of the terrors of the night, nor the arrow that flies in the day. Do not dread the disease that stalks in darkness, nor the disaster that strikes at midday. Though a thousand fall at your side, though ten thousand are dying around you, these evils will not touch you." (Ps. 91:1–7 NLT)

I looked up the word "fear" in the *New Strong's Expanded Exhaustive Concordance of the Bible* and there are 404 references found in the King James Version. Some of those count toward fearing the Lord, which simply means to respect and revere him. But I think it's safe to say there are a lot of reminders calling God's people to not be afraid. Isn't it fair to assume that God knew we would need that many reminders because it is only human to fear? In other words, fear is in our fleshly nature. We will spend a lifetime on this earth learning the love of God, which casts out fear. Since we are still learning, we will struggle with fear, worry, anxiety, and even depression in seasons. The goal isn't to cultivate a life free of fear; such a life doesn't exist. It's to learn how to fear less. Until we fully understand the perfect love of God, which can't wholly happen until we are in glory with him in heaven, we will still struggle with fear and anxiety. Since we are humans who are constantly works in progress, doesn't it make sense that we might need some help along the way? What if that help comes in the form of medication?

Let's tackle the big question: Does God approve of medication to treat mental health conditions? Because my body was in fight-or-flight mode, and since there was a flood of cortisol and adrenaline coursing through me, the fight-or-flight stress response was active. Long-term activation of this stress response mode was what got me in trouble. Sometimes our bodies can get stuck in this mode for various reasons; mine was due to lack of rest and over-working. The consequences of my behavior created physical and chemical responses, which triggered panic attacks. At the same time, the happy messengers in my brain, dopamine and serotonin, were radically out of balance as well. Consequently, my mental health was affected, and I began to experience depression and suicidal thoughts.

Our body needs balance; too much or too little of something will create problems. Imagine a teeter-totter; if only one person is on it, the enjoyment of bouncing up and down can never happen. Another person joining the teeter-totter will balance out the fun. My body was like a teeter-totter with only one person; I was severely out of balance. The chemical responses triggered by countless years of overworking and striving put me at a point in life where nothing was enjoyable. At that moment, I had a choice: believe in a supernatural miracle from God to heal my dangerously out-of-balance body, or let medication be the thing that joined my teeter-totter to help me get the balance back. Surprisingly, I found that the answer didn't need to be either/or, it could be both. You can believe in miracles while taking practical steps toward healing.

I believe God could have wiped away every panic attack I endured. He could have healed my out-of-balance body, restored my happy messengers, and stabilized the overflowing amounts of adrenaline and cortisol because he is a God that is still in the business of providing miracles. I also believe that sometimes God will take us through a problem to understand a promise he wants to instill in us. That's precisely what happened in my story; I faced problems and learned God's promises. You will find God's promises declared throughout the pages of this book. Even though I didn't receive the miracle of healing from panic and anxiety disorder overnight, there were many mini-miracles along the way, mini-miracles that were activated by the prayers of my husband, friends, and family, as well as my own prayers.

## Take the Medication

My doctor advised me to take medicine to balance the physical and chemical responses in my body. I remember my friend, who had been through this already, urging me to take the drugs that would be helpful. Yet, something in me just didn't want to comply. I was scared this would be my forever. I didn't want to rely on medication for the rest of my life. Part of it was a lack of understanding of how the drugs worked, and another part was just pure pride.

The superwoman I was used to operating as didn't need medication, yet the weak and panicking woman I was now living as felt like I needed it. The struggle was real. Do I take medicine or not?

It took me a while to discover this, but the way I see it now, medication is a gift from God. James 1:17 notes that "every good and perfect gift is from above" (CSB). God allows medications to be a part of our stories here on earth. We live in a fallen and broken world, which means sickness and diseases will be a part of that journey. If medication provides a means to healing, then why wouldn't we take that blessing? No one thinks twice about a cancer patient taking the medication called chemotherapy or the person with diabetes taking their insulin shots. We know those medications aid in providing a prolonged life or even healing. So why do we struggle to believe anxiety and depression medications won't do the same? Maybe it's because we lack understanding of where faith and mental health medications should intersect.

Taking medication does not mean you lack faith. I will write it again for the person abused by a spiritual giant who led you to believe otherwise: taking medication does not mean you lack faith. Now that I have made that abundantly clear, I have a confession: I think antianxiety and antidepression medications are highly overprescribed. There is a time and a place for these drugs; my story is a prime example of that necessary and meaningful intervention. I couldn't function to complete routine activities. A shower was a task I often struggled to achieve.

Without the help of medication, I wouldn't have been able to return to everyday life to work on my physical, spiritual, and mental health. Medicine played a massive role in my wellness and recovery, and for that, I am forever grateful to God.

Unfortunately, many people turn to medication to mask pressure and pain instead of dealing with their problems. Medication should not be a Band-Aid to cover up what is happening in your life. That approach is not healthy or wise. Dr. Caroline Leaf explains in *Cleaning up Your Mental Mess*:

> Anxiety, depression, burnout, frustration, angst, anger, grief, and so on are emotional and physical warning signals telling us we need to face and deal with something that's happened or is happening in our life. This pain, which is very *real*, is a sign that there's something wrong: you are in a state of disequilibrium. It's not a sign of a defective brain. Your experience doesn't need to be validated by a medical label. Mental health struggles are not your identity. They're normal and need to be addressed, not suppressed, or things will get worse.[6]

My wise primary care doctor, upon diagnosing me with severe panic and anxiety disorder, told me something similar. "Christy, I'm going to prescribe you some medication. It's going to help you. But if you don't get to the root of your problem, your medication will have to be increased regularly. That pattern will continue over the years. It will be best to seek wise counsel to figure out how you got into this situation."

My take from my doctor's infinite wisdom was that I had work to do. But isn't it so much easier to just take the pill or, in my case, pills? Sure, it might have been easier just to take the pills and go about my business, but the part that haunted me was when the doctor said it would never be enough. The dosage would just keep increasing through the years. I didn't want that for my life, and if a doctor told you the same thing, I believe that you wouldn't want that either. But the truth is that most people don't want to put in the work to dig deep and find out why they are struggling mentally. Digging deep is a painful process. Sometimes you must go backward to plow forward. An arrow on a bow needs to be pulled back to find the speed and strength to fly. So does the arrow of your life.

## The Counseling Connection

I believe in therapy—Christian therapy, that is. Please follow me closely because this can get tricky. Many great therapists are not Christian. The process with a non-Christian therapist can be very effective, but I believe it can only get you so far. My friend Rachel Elmore, an author, speaker, and owner of a Christian counseling practice, explains it this way:

> I use the same tools and techniques that any secular therapist would use in a counseling practice. I have the same training as a secular therapist. In many ways, it's not that different. However, there's one significant difference between the two. Secular therapy bases its treatment on theory. Many Christian counselors use theory and truth—the truth of what God says about us and our actions. Now, theory matters a lot. However, for many Christian counselors, truth and the Word of God matter more than theory. Truth trumps theory.
>
> Now, there's nothing wrong with seeing a secular therapist. I personally would not because I want my therapist to understand the role of my faith in my life, my health, and my decisions.
>
> But I don't tell people to do what feels good. I tell people to do what is right. If you do what is right, He will honor that, and God will be glorified.[7]

I completely agree with Rachel. Truth trumps theory. As I mentioned in Chapter Three, our moral compass must point to the absolute truth of God for us to walk in true freedom. As I got to know God's truth in my life, it transformed me from the inside out.

Only the power of God's Word packed with truth can do that, and theory does not even come in a close second.

I hold the personal belief that anyone who takes medication for anxiety or depression should be in therapy, too. Medicine is not a Band-Aid; it's a tool. Therefore, when anxiety or depression medication is prescribed, it is best to pair it with therapy. After being diagnosed with severe panic and anxiety disorder, I went through eighteen months of intensive Christian therapy. If you believe the Bible that we are spirit, soul, and body, then therapy is the doctor for our soul. We visit our doctors for yearly checkups to take care of our bodies (well, some do). Couldn't we extend that same level of importance to our souls, which is our source of mental health? I realize women especially have a hard time caring for themselves. I dedicated a whole section of this book in the next chapter to why self-care is biblical.

Do you know the old children's toy called a jack-in-the-box? You wind it up, it plays some circus-sounding music, and "Jack" pops out when you least expect it. Our souls are being wound up daily like a jack-in-the-box through conflicts, trials, suffering, and opposition. It's just how life goes. The hard part is that we "pop out" at some point. That can look like anxiety, depression, panic, and fear. The goal of therapy is to work through it so we don't get wound up so tightly and pop. When we do pop, it's even more vital to seek Christian counseling. To be proactive instead of reactive with therapy is even better.

A monthly check-in seems to be a good rhythm for me. Finding a good therapist can be challenging. Generally, the local church you attend is a good starting place. Word of mouth is also very effective; ask your circle of friends. Post on your social media feeds or private groups that you want to find a therapist. It is important to note that I didn't end up with the same counselor for the entire eighteen months of recovery. It took me a while to find one who matched my needs. Even today, I'm not with the same one. As my life as a leader changed, so did the requirements I was looking for in a Christian therapist. Advocate for yourself to find the right counseling match.

In the quote I shared, Leaf beautifully points out that anxiety, depression, burnout, frustration, angst, anger, and grief are natural for our bodies to feel. So, what do we do with all those emotions? In the next chapter, we are going to talk about smoke alarms. The body naturally sends these warning signals when something is wrong. Should we choose to press into these warning signs instead of ignoring them, preventing a nervous breakdown may be possible. Should you find yourself at nervous breakdown status, I hope you feel less shame and more peace about taking anxiety and depression pills.

A final word on medication: it is not God. You should never run to it before you run to him. Once I started making progress over panic after my medication started, it would have been easy to trust the medicine as my healer. That is a dangerous trap. My hope and foundation are in Jesus, not Celexa. Putting medication on a pedestal will create far more fear and anxiety in your life. Why? Because it's not the ultimate answer. Jesus is the answer. He is the life, the truth, and the way. In him, you will find all the answers you need, and you may find that those answers include medication.

Jesus, seeing a doctor, and Christian therapy are the top three things I credit that helped me overcome severe panic and anxiety disorder. It took eighteen months to get to a point where I felt like a normal, functioning, productive adult. It took me years to get into that mess; I'm grateful it only took me eighteen months to get out of it. The point is to have grace with your healing process. Don't rush it, and don't delay it either.

Maybe it's wishful thinking, but I believe the church and the medical community want to do better. More education and awareness around mental health disorders would benefit both worlds greatly. You can start by asking your church if they would consult with your Christian counselor. Bridging that gap could be the start of something beautiful. We are not aiding anyone to freedom by discounting mental health concerns and telling them just to read the Bible and pray more.

Additionally, we are not doing any favors by telling them just to pop a pill; addressing the person's body, soul, and spirit matters. I believe this so strongly that I dream of starting a soul center, which has been on my vision board for years. I see pieces of the soul center starting to come together. God willing, one day, I will lead a facility where a person gets treated as three parts and with one outcome: freedom!

## NOTES

[1] Caroline Leaf, *Cleaning Up Your Mental Mess* (Grand Rapids: Baker, 2021), 15.

[2] Stephen M. Rappaport, "Genetic Factors Are Not the Major Causes of Chronic Diseases," *PLoS ONE* 11, no. 4 (April 2016), quoted in Leaf, *Cleaning Up Your Mental Mess*, 52.

[3] SAVE: Suicide Awareness Voices of Education, "Suicide Statistics: 2020 Global Statistics," SAVE, accessed Nov. 7, 2022, https://save.org/about-suicide/suicide-statistics/#:~:text=Nearly%20800%2C000%20people%20die%20by,leading%20cause%20of%20disability%20worldwide.

[4] George H. Pember, *Earth's Earliest Ages* (Grand Rapids: Kregel, 1942), 77, quoted in John Woodward, "Man As Spirit, Soul, and Body," chap. 3, *Grace Notebook*, https://gracenotebook.com/man-as-spirit-soul-and-body-chapter-3/.

[5] Chris Morris, *Whispers in the Pews: Voices on Mental Illness in the Church* (Chicago: Llama Publishing, 2018), 63.

[6] Leaf, *Cleaning Up Your Mental Mess*, 17.

[7] Rachel Elmore, text to author.

# CHAPTER 5

# Smoke Alarms

Not too long ago, we had a minor flood in our bathroom that leaked into our basement through the air vent. Once we got the water cleaned up on both floors, the smoke alarm started going off. Water damage, not smoke, shorted it out. Yet, we couldn't ignore it. Smoke alarms are annoying for a reason. Once activated, they want you to act immediately for your safety and protection. Once an alarm goes off in your house, you put a plan of action into place. This chapter will help you identify anxiety smoke alarms and will inspire you to act quickly once your body sets them off.

In the case of a real-life fire, first, you assess the situation. Next, you care for yourself and then your loved ones. Third, you call for help. Last, you remove yourself from the situation. I will walk all those steps out practically as they pertain to anxiety, but first, I like to think that our bodies also have built-in smoke alarm systems. When my body starts feeling any of these smoke alarms:

- Fast or irregular heartbeat
- Chest tightness and heaviness
- Upset stomach, nausea, or diarrhea
- Shortness of breath
- Weakness or dizziness
- Feeling hot or cold
- Tingly or numb limbs, especially in arms and hands
- Hives or itchy spots on the skin
- Hair loss
- Tension headaches
- Clenched or sore jaw
- Severe insomnia
- Racing, uncontrollable thoughts

I treat it as though there is a fire I need to put out. It is unwise to ignore your body's smoke alarms. Sometimes you find it's just a little smoke, and other times you may find a major fire brewing. Smoke alarms are built-in blessings, and we must begin paying attention to them.

Having occasional anxiety is a normal part of life. However, repeated anxiety that does not get addressed becomes dangerous, like what happened to me. The doctors diagnosed me with severe panic disorder and anxiety. Despite smoke alarms going off for years, I had no understanding of the damage I did to myself. It is my hope that this chapter will be the catalyst that motivates you not to silence your smoke alarms anymore.

It's important to note that I am not a medical professional. I indeed have a lot of experience with panic and anxiety, but it is always wise to run your symptoms by a doctor. I am writing about my own experience in hopes that you will learn from it. Everyone's body reacts differently when panic and anxiety are present. Resist the urge to compare anxiety stories, and always take your physician and clinical team's advice over mine. However, it is essential to advocate for yourself. Often, you will know your body better than a physician will. You must lean into that. Education and knowledge are powerful assets when dealing with your anxiety symptoms. The Holy Spirit is working through you as well.

We all have different thresholds for stress. Just as a car can go different lengths of times before the engine blows due to not changing the oil, it's the same for our bodies. If the vehicle is older and has had more wear and tear, it might need an oil change sooner than a newer model. The threshold for a breakdown in the body depends on the wear and tear and how we manage stress. You have warning lights that go off in your car when something is not correct, and you care for that signal when you see it go off. The same is true for the smoke alarms in our bodies.

When a smoke alarm presents itself, I first try ways to reduce the stress response naturally. Low-impact exercise, proper diet, therapy, taking negative thoughts captive, essential oils, worship, prayer, and reading the Bible have proven to be tremendously helpful. But those are proactive and preventative measures, not cures once your body is shutting down from repeated and long-standing stress.

## Smoke Alarm Steps

When you notice a smoke alarm, first, assess the situation. What are your symptoms? You should never ignore chest pain or heaviness, a racing heartbeat, or frequent painful heart palpitations. If you have never experienced those symptoms before, take those smoke alarms straight to the emergency room. Since I have been checked out by medical professionals numerous times with those symptoms and came up healthy, I know those smoke alarms mean that I have overdone it. Chest tightness and heaviness are usually among my first smoke alarms when I feel anxious. Generally, my biggest clue is when my chest feels tight, like a rubber band is being stretched across it. To silence that alarm, I typically take time to do some deep breathing and go on a walk. Excess stress hormones get burned while walking. It's helpful to get your heart rate up with easy exercise. It is best not to do a full-blown exercise routine when anxiety is already high; however, raising your heart rate with moderate walking can help, and it always does for me. Then, I rest, pray, and put on some worship music. When I pay attention to chest tightness and heaviness as a smoke alarm, it usually subsides quickly.

When I first experienced panic and anxiety, I lost my hair because my adrenal glands suffered from prolonged stress. Several years later, hair loss was a sign that my thyroid was not working correctly. I needed extra clinical attention for that symptom, which required blood work. The doctor looked at my T3 and T4 plus TSH (total thyroid-stimulating hormone) to determine if my thyroid was working right. They also tested for something not commonly tested for in traditional medicine (at least it wasn't common for me) called thyroid peroxidase (TPO). The presence of this antibody indicates an autoimmune disorder like Hashimoto's disease or Graves' disease. Surprisingly, Hashimoto's is more common than you might think. I tested positive for Hashimoto's, so anxiety can sometimes mean my thyroid is off again. I'm very aware of my physical symptoms, which is extremely helpful when navigating my health as it pertains to my body, soul, and spirit.

I could write a whole book about my journey with Hashimoto's, but I will summarize it in a few sentences. Nutrition and exercise matter. Our gut is said to be our second brain. If our gut is not healthy, it can trigger anxiety and other health conditions. With proper testing, through the help of a functional medicine doctor,

I found out that my gut has many issues. Learning how to heal it with nutrition and supplements has been a game changer. I have seen an extreme difference for the better after I started a paleo lifestyle, cut out caffeine, and incorporated at least thirty minutes of exercise per day. Most of the time, that exercise looks like a brisk walk. My primary care doctor practices with an emphasis in functional medicine, and because of that, I have seen significant improvements in my overall health. My prayer is that we will see more practitioners recognizing the importance of functional medicine. Until then, advocate for yourself. Tell your traditional medicine doctor that you want to explore more holistic ways of healing and that you want to get to the root cause of the problem. I'm so grateful I found a primary care physician who practices using functional medicine methods. I prayed and asked God for wisdom to guide me to find a doctor like this. God is faithful to provide when you trust him.

Gastrointestinal issues like diarrhea are smoke alarms that sound off when I am in the heat of an anxiety attack. Anxiety releases chemicals in the body that disrupt the gastrointestinal tract, and the response can be diarrhea, an upset stomach that can cause vomiting, or in some cases, even constipation. You have all heard of the saying, "I have butterflies in my stomach." That is the language behind what's happening in our stomachs when we feel anxious. The response is often not much fun in the bathroom. Remember my Hardee's story from Chapter Two? When these smoke alarms come up, I have to ride out the storm until it passes. Once it does, I give myself some time to rebound and make sure I replenish with lots of water and rest.

Tight muscles, tension headaches, and a clenched jaw are major smoke alarms for me. When your body's fight-or-flight response is activated, the natural reaction is muscle tightness. A good time to take inventory of body tension is while you're lying in bed. I will often catch myself clenching my jaw and raising my shoulders instead of relaxing. Often at night, I will realize that my back and neck are sore, too. Remember the saying, "You're a pain in the neck"? It simply means you are stressing me out. Stress has significant effects on our bodies. I also hold a lot of tension in my shoulder blades, and when I'm stressed, my back is full of knots. Get a massage if you're not sure where you hold your tension. A good massage therapist can tell you exactly where the tension is. The bonus is that a massage helps reduce stress and anxiety. If you can't afford regular massages, manufacturers make great massage guns these days. I just bought two for my sons so they can massage their sore muscles after a tough week of sports. You better believe I use those guns regularly to work on my tense muscles.

Racing thoughts and insomnia are also alarms. In Chapter Seven, I will tell you, step-by-step, how to stop racing thoughts. When your mind is racing, you can't sleep. When you can't sleep, you can't restore, and when you are tired, you can't respond to stressful situations well. Then you enter a vicious circle of stress. If you want to sleep well, you need to calm your mind. Also, when I overcommit, I get insomnia. Being so busy that you can't get the recommended seven to nine hours of sleep isn't a cool thing; if I may be so bold, it's a stupid thing. Some people think they can tolerate less sleep, and they are fooling themselves. Lack of sleep is a breeding ground for anxiety. Insomnia isn't healthy; I hope you feel convicted to take seriously the smoke alarm of insomnia and the number of hours of sleep you are getting.

During a severe panic attack, my body experiences tingling sensations that can linger even afterward. Sometimes if something scary happens to me, I can feel the jolt of adrenalin running through my body, resulting in tingling in my limbs. For example, if I slam on my brakes because someone cuts me off, I can feel pins and needles flood my arms, my hands, and sometimes my legs.

That can be a normal response, but if that tingling stays around too long, it can mean that your body is stuck in fight-or-flight, and you should pay attention to that smoke alarm and see a doctor.

Skin irritations like hives are common when anxiety and stress are present. Usually, these smoke alarms will occur if I'm doing a speaking event or walking into a challenging conversation that includes conflict. The stress hormones are activated in these situations because of nerves, and they cause my skin to react in funny ways. Generally, my skin returns to normal after the circumstance is over and my body is calm.

Shortness of breath, weakness, or dizziness happens when the stress response gets activated in my body. You must remember that everything, including your heart, must work harder in your body when you are under stress. If you are short of breath, your body may not be getting enough oxygen, which can make you feel weak and dizzy. Have you heard of the brown paper bag breathing trick? This technique is when you put a brown paper bag over your mouth and breathe into it. There is nothing special about the bag; it's just a focus point for concentrating on your breathing. Slow, deep breaths can lower the stress response happening in your body. I don't respond well to the brown paper bag trick. However, a box fan on high during a panic attack works wonders for me. I put my face in front of the fan, and the strong air coming at me forces me to take deep breaths. It works like a charm.

Take a moment to do a smoke alarm inventory on yourself. Which of these smoke alarms have you experienced in the last month? Circle all that apply:

- Fast or irregular heartbeat
- Chest tightness and heaviness
- Upset stomach, nausea, or diarrhea
- Shortness of breath

- Weakness or dizziness
- Feeling hot or cold
- Tingly or numb limbs, especially in arms and hands
- Hives or itchy spots on the skin
- Hair loss
- Tension headaches
- Clenched or sore jaw
- Severe insomnia
- Racing, uncontrollable thoughts
- _____ (other)

## Help Yourself before You Help Others

When a smoke alarm goes off, the next step is to care for yourself and _then_ your loved ones. Before a crash on an airplane, the flight attendant usually tells you to put on your oxygen mask before helping someone else. We are worthless to others if we are not first caring for ourselves. What would be the point of helping someone with their oxygen before putting on your oxygen mask before a plane crash? It may seem like a bold and courageous thing, but it's not the most effective option. You will be able to help someone for a few minutes before you pass out from lack of oxygen, but you would be able to help so many more people if you first took care of yourself. I have found, especially in Christian circles, that we don't want to care for ourselves because it can appear selfish. I turn to Jesus's examples when I start to believe the lie that self-care is not holy. Scripture mentions specific instances when he rested, refueled, and cared for his soul so he could help others effectively.

A bold move by Jesus was when he went into the wilderness for forty days and nights, as recorded in Matthew and Luke. After being baptized by John and being called into public ministry, Jesus went to the wilderness to pray alone. When is the last time you took a break to be alone for forty days and nights? Any time God calls us into something big, it is wise to take time to get alone with God. Far too often, we rush into things and wind up depleting ourselves of energy that God never asked us to spend. I am encouraged that the most excellent leader and human of all time carved out space to be alone with God. Time alone with God cannot be taken away by the pressures of this world. You might be thinking I have gone mad for even suggesting forty days and nights alone with God, because you can't even get four minutes alone. Maybe it can't be a full forty days, but how would your life change for the better if you stopped to take seven days to be alone with God? If you can't do seven, start smaller with three days. If you can't do three, then do one day. And just in case you are wondering if caring for his soul was just a one-off thing Jesus decided to do before he went into public ministry, here is some proof that Jesus made withdrawing a habit: "But Jesus often withdrew to the wilderness for prayer" (Luke 5:16 NLT). How often do you withdraw? My hunch is not often enough.

Jesus also encouraged soul rest before making a major decision. "One day soon afterward Jesus went up on a mountain to pray, and he prayed to God all night. At daybreak he called together all of his disciples and chose twelve of them to be apostles" (Luke 6:12–13 NLT). We see that Jesus did two specific things in choosing the twelve apostles. One, he got away from people. Two, he prayed for an extended period. Traveling to the top of a mountain is not convenient. Therefore, it made it hard for people to find him. What if we were more intentional at hiding from people to get wisdom, rest, and peace our souls need so that we can handle the people God has entrusted to us? Then, what if we used that time wisely in prayer instead of wasting it on Netflix and mindlessly scrolling on social media?

Heartache and sorrow are inevitable parts of life. If you are not careful, these emotions, while healthy, will suck the life out of you, especially if you don't slow down to be with God. What I love about the example Jesus set for us is that he walked through hardships, too. He isn't a stuffy high priest who just commands us to do things without experiencing them himself. His actions leading up to or following distress were remarkable. By being alone and praying during troubled times, he took care of his soul. Below are two scriptures that show us what he did in times of sorrow. The first example is after he got the news that a beheading killed his dear friend and cousin John the Baptist. The disciples delivered the information, and Scripture says, ". . . he left in a boat to a remote area to be alone" (Matt. 14:13 NLT). Sorrow takes a lot out of you. Taking time to be alone and process your grief is necessary. We cannot just hide from our pain. We must process it with God.

Nearing the end of his ministry, Jesus experienced severe distress. Knowing that his time on the cross was about to begin, Jesus got away to pray. Do you see a pattern? "He walked away, about a stone's throw, and knelt down and prayed, 'Father, if you are willing, please take this cup of suffering away from me. Yet I want your will to be done, not mine'" (Luke 22:41–42 NLT). He prayed a specific and heartfelt prayer to God.

The subsequent soul care Jesus requested is quite possibly my favorite example:

> The apostles returned to Jesus from their ministry tour and told him all they had done and taught. Then Jesus said, "Let's go off by ourselves to a quiet place and rest awhile." He said this because there were so many people coming and going that Jesus and his apostles didn't even have time to eat. So they left by boat for a quiet place, where they could be alone. (Mark 6:30–32 NLT)

I have put my life circumstances into these scriptures before. It plays out like this:

"Jesus, guess what? The Fearless team hosted a retreat where many women got freed up and are following you now. We worshiped and prayed earnestly for a breakthrough, and you delivered them! I found it exhausting but rewarding at the same time. Then I spoke at a conference for two days and saw walls break down. I prayed for over 250 women, many of whom came to me with their brokenness and heavy hearts. We sought you, and chains of fear and anxiety fell. I had over a hundred messages that I needed to process in email, Facebook, and Instagram when I got home. But now that I'm home, it's time to love my family. My husband is struggling with grief. We cried and held each other as we processed the pain in our hearts from losing our loved ones. Then my daughter needed help with some friendship issues. So, we spent some time together talking about being a good friend and how to stand up against bullies. My middle son struggles with his faith. He told me scary things about how the devil whispered lies to him. We spent time learning how to build faith and take our thoughts captive. Then, my oldest son is trying to figure out his future. I'm encouraging him to seek you in all he does and not get caught up in the world's way of doing things, but I'm concerned that I'm not doing enough to help him see that."

Then Jesus said to me, "Let's go off by ourselves to a quiet place and rest awhile. You have a lot going on right now, too many people coming and going, and you can't even take time to eat. Let's find a quiet place to be alone."

Jesus is calling you to do the same thing, as his words are to everyone. Our works are not greater than our relationship with Jesus.

God created us to love him with our hearts, souls, and minds. Out of that overflow, then we share God's love with people. Is it possible that you are too busy helping people? Did Jesus ask you to do all the helping you are doing? Leading others to find and follow Jesus is part of the Great Commission, but we must never forget that spending time in solitude with God to refresh our souls is not selfish; it is necessary to survive. In managing anxiety smoke alarms, first work on your relationship with Jesus, and then you will be in a position to help others.

There are times when you cannot stop the smoke alarms because an actual fire has broken out. It would be foolish for you to ignore the fire and walk away. You would never do that if your house were burning down. You would call for help, and that's the third step. Sometimes, anxiety can feel overwhelming. Calling in reinforcements is not only wise; it is crucial. Sometimes this help comes in the form of a physician or counselor. Sometimes it comes through the help of a dear friend, spouse, or pastor. In Chapter Eight, I will walk you through ways to get help when dealing with anxiety.

Let's review the steps: Assess the situation, help yourself before you help others, call for help, and remove yourself from the situation. The last step is crucial when it comes to paying attention to smoke alarms. Many of us stay in burning buildings for far too long. Being in a toxic friendship that caused me brutal amounts of anxiety is an example of staying in a burning building for too long. I had many smoke alarms going off, and as I assessed the situation, all signs pointed to being in an unhealthy relationship. I badly wanted things to change because I cared deeply for my friend. However, they didn't get better. They only got worse. After praying and seeking wisdom from God, I stumbled upon a beautiful verse:

Therefore, since we are surrounded by such a huge crowd of witnesses to the life of faith, let us strip off every weight that slows us down, especially the sin that so easily trips us up. And let us run with endurance the race God has set before us. (Heb. 12:1 NLT)

Your circle of influence matters. My mentor Kristin Bonin says, "You must choose wisely who you pull closely." Not everyone will support or champion the dreams and desires God has given you to accomplish. It gets heavy having to explain yourself to naysayers, especially if those naysayers are dear friends. That's why you must not do that. It's hard enough to run this race called life. Run it with a cloud of witnesses who want to see you succeed and who believe in what God is calling you to do. We do this by stripping off every weight that is slowing us down.

## Conflict Is a Trigger for Stress and Anxiety

After much prayer and support from my husband, I took what I felt the Lord was calling me to do with this friendship to wise counsel. I finally made the vital decision to remove myself from the situation. I had a difficult time ending our friendship. I realized the friendship was a burden I was carrying around that I didn't have to carry, and it was burning me up. It took bravery to leave behind the things burning up my soul, but the result was a tremendous amount of peace. Any loss of peace you may be experiencing must be evaluated and brought to Jesus. My only regret in this situation is I wish I had listened to those smoke alarms sooner.

Many of the people I speak with are constantly dealing with smoke alarms because of conflicts at work. People put off conflict more in work environments because they fear losing their job, so they put up with unhealthy circumstances for much longer.

Conflict is a top trigger for stress and anxiety. To work through conflict, you need to assess the situation in a healthy way to determine if you need to leave.

Below are the steps I take when conflict arises in the workforce. I have developed these steps straight out of Matthew 18:15–17. It is true that Matthew 18 talks about correcting another believer in a church context. Still, in my experience, these steps have worked tremendously well, even when I'm dealing with people who are not believers. Remember, refusing to hit conflict head-on and quickly will keep smoke alarms going off regularly.

1.  If you are in conflict with someone, request a private meeting. The worst mistake made during arguments is making a spectacle out of something that should be kept private. Be clear and concise on why you are hurt and what you would like to see happen moving forward. Be humble and open to areas you can improve in as well.
2.  If the first step does not bring resolution, ask for a mediator to be present, and work through Step 1 again.
3.  If the second step doesn't work, you can bring your case to a higher authority, like a boss over the person you're in conflict with or the human resources department.

If there is no resolution after Step 3, it's time to remove yourself from the situation prayerfully. The cost to your health of staying in a toxic environment for far too long is not worth it. God would not want you to stay in an unhealthy situation either, especially if you have remained humble and have walked through all the proper steps to resolve the conflict. There are times when peace won't be possible because the other person is unwilling to act peacefully. Then I recommend we lean into this powerful promise: "If it is possible, as far as it depends on you, live at peace with everyone"

(Rom. 12:18 NIV). You do your best, and let God do the rest. When forced to leave a toxic work environment, we must trust him.

I have given you four steps to take when smoke alarms start sounding: assess the situation, care for yourself and then your loved ones, call for help, and remove yourself from the situation. The truth is, most of this is much easier said than done. Smoke alarms are tricky. There is a temptation to ignore them or even put them on snooze. We do this because we don't think individual warnings are that important. I can tell you from firsthand experience that they are important! Now you have the awareness I wish I had in 2011 before my nervous breakdown. I ignored many smoke alarms through the years, and I regret it. I don't want you to have smoke alarm laments too. You have a choice: ignore or listen to the blessing of your body's built-in smoke alarms. Ignorance is not bliss. Prompt attention to your smoke alarms will help you become healthier in every aspect of your life.

# CHAPTER 6

# Perfect Love Casts Out Fear

In the most extraordinary love story ever written, God sacrificed his one and only son so we could gain eternal life. Can such an unconditional love truly exist—a perfect heaven-born love, not an imperfect earthbound love? Our human minds have a hard time grasping this kind of love. We only know human love. But the love of God? It's far more remarkable. Take a moment to read this love letter written for you:

*Sweet child of mine. Before the earth was even formed, I knew you. I knitted you together perfectly in your mother's womb. I have fearfully and wonderfully made you. I have mighty plans for your life, plans to prosper you and not harm you. I make no mistakes; my works are perfect. I know you so intimately that I have numbered the hairs on your head. Do your most intimate loved ones know that about you? You have no thought or idea that I don't already know about. My love for you is unconditional and is not based on your love for me. My love for you is as deep as the ocean and outnumbers the grains of sand, and still, that doesn't even begin to explain my never-ending, steadfast love for you. I sent my only son to die for you so you could have everlasting life. My perfect love for you casts out fear. There is nothing, absolutely nothing, that can separate you from my love. I will be back again someday to get you. Until then, live loved. Live in peace. Live fearlessly.*

*Love,*
*God*

Although this letter was my human attempt to capture the heart of God, I hope you read every word carefully and soaked in its meaning. The sentences woven together are promises from his Word. You can take this letter at face value and believe it. Take a picture of it, and make it your screen saver. Text it to a friend, post it on social media, tell the world that God loves you, and remind somebody else that he loves them too.

What does God's love have to do with fear? A lot. Until I truly learned to rest in God's love, I continued to struggle significantly with fear and anxiety, which leads me to ask: Can understanding his love be a method we've overlooked in overcoming anxiety? I believe strongly that our world has massively overlooked understanding God's love as a method of overcoming anxiety. What does Scripture teach about how the two are connected? We need to explore God's love and how it casts out our fears, and that's what this chapter is all about.

You may have had a hard time with the love letter if, deep down, you struggle on some level with truly comprehending God's love. I feel that a fair number of people, including myself, would say they have been taught that God loves them, but it's hard to believe how much or why. God is love, and God loves us. Yet, we don't always buy it. There are many different reasons why we might question God's love. Does any of this sound familiar to you?

- There are so many bad things happening in our world, God can't possibly be love.
- There are so many bad things happening to me, God can't possibly love me.
- I have made so many bad decisions, God can't love me.
- There are so many people in this world, God can't possibly love us all.

There is likely something blocking you from fully walking in the freedom of God's love, so please slowly read and absorb the following sentences. Your pain, your story, and your life experiences are seen. You are the apple of God's eye. He sees you. You are valuable. You are important. You are worthy. Every tear you have cried has not gone unnoticed. You have a God who loves you.

## Depth and Magnitude

Now, let's dive deep into God's love for us. I asked God in prayer to help me adequately explain his love. I felt the words *depth* and *magnitude* come to my heart. Let's look at the first word, *depth*, and its definition. A simple lexicon search revealed many ways to define *depth*; three definitions struck me the most: "[1] The distance from the nearest to the farthest point of something. [2] The quality of being intense or extreme, or complexity and profundity of thought. [3] A point far below the surface."

Let's look at the first explanation, "the distance from the nearest to the farthest point of something," and see the correlation from God's Word. "He does not punish us for all our sins; he does not deal harshly with us, as we deserve. For his unfailing love

85

toward those who fear him is as great as the height of the heavens above the earth. He has removed our sins as far from us as the east is from the west" (Ps. 103:10–12 NLT). His love is as far, deep, wide, and high as you can possibly go. It's as great as the height of the heavens above the earth. His love has no boundary. If that isn't deep enough, the scripture continues with some more depth. "He has removed our sins as far . . . as the east is from the west." Not only is his love deep, but his forgiveness for your sins is deeper. That's a crazy type of amazing love.

Let's look at the second definition of *depth*: intense or extreme quality or complexity and profundity of thought. I must pause for a moment to hopefully allow you to laugh. Have you ever heard the word *profundity*? I mean, it sounds made up. When I looked up *profundity* on Google, I had to play the sound bite so I knew how to pronounce it. I couldn't write about a word I didn't know how to say. Anyway, I digress. What does this have to do with depth and God's love? Check this out: "'For my thoughts are not your thoughts, neither are your ways my ways,' declares the LORD. 'As the heavens are higher than the earth, so are my ways higher than your ways and my thoughts than your thoughts'" (Isa. 55:8–9 NIV). The Bible perfectly illustrates the double whammy of depth. I believe this scripture is saying that God's ways are complex and profound. In other words, God has deep insight, a great depth of knowledge that we can't even begin to understand. His ways are higher, better, and may even feel extreme at times. Why? Because God is God, and we are not. Sometimes the simple yet profound answer to your questions and trials in life is that God's ways are higher.

Breaking down *depth* a little further, it means an extensive and detailed amount of knowledge. If you're going to trust someone, don't you want them to know what they are doing? God is all-knowing. "And the very hairs of your head are all numbered. So don't be afraid; you are more valuable to God than a whole flock of sparrows" (Luke 12:7 NLT). Wait—do you know precisely how many hairs are on your head? Many of us are sporting hair extensions, too, so that's extra hair! To know every hair on your head is extreme. Who knows you that well? Not your husband, not your kids, not your parents, not your best friend, not your dog—just God. He is the only one with that extreme depth of knowledge.

The last part of the *depth* definition is a point far below the surface, the worst or lowest part or state. God's depth goes deep enough to understand our pain and lowest state. How do we know that? "So then, since we have a great High Priest who has entered heaven, Jesus the Son of God, let us hold firmly to what we believe. This High Priest of ours understands our weaknesses, for he faced all of the same testings we do, yet he did not sin" (Heb. 4:14–15 NLT). The writer of Hebrews brings up some big thoughts with profundity, so let's back up. The "High Priest" means Jesus. He offered himself for our sins once and for all so we can have eternal life. You kind of win the title of High Priest when you do that for all humankind, you know? But look what it says next that is ever so deep. He "understands our weaknesses, for he faced all of the same testings we do, yet he did not sin."

Allow me some liberties to work this out a bit. Jesus didn't scream at his children when the "stress balloon" filled with kitchen flour exploded all over his car. Oh, wait, I did that. He didn't cuss at his family members when they caught him in a stressful moment. Oh wait, that was me. He didn't get drunk on wine and preach to the waitress at the dinner table. Embarrassingly, me again. (Don't judge too hard; God has convicted me since on drunkenness, and that doesn't happen anymore). All liberties aside, he understands your most profound, darkest moments and everyday mess-ups. He had offers set before him to mess up and sin, too; he just didn't. He handled temptations way better than you and I do. Doesn't that make you love and respect him so much more? We don't serve a super stuffy high God that never felt pain or invitations to sin. It's reassuring that God understands our pain, sorrows, trials, and temptations.

Let's move on to *magnitude*. The Latin root of *magnitude*, *magnitūdō*, means "greatness of character." Let's just stop for a second and ponder the profundity of God again. Are you like, *Wow, is this for real?* Truthfully, I had no way to know that the original Latin root word of *magnitude* meant "greatness of character." I'm not that book smart, and my ACT test score can prove that. When I felt the Lord whisper *depth* and *magnitude* to help depict his love for us, that experience alone showed his great character. Each of us can hear from God, and hearing from God is part of learning his great nature.

What do we see if we look at God's magnitude or character? The great size or extent of something. Generally, large or more extensive things are considered valuable. You pay attention to anything worthwhile in life. When your stocks are valuable, you turn your attention to them. Your phone is valuable, so you pay a lot of attention to it. Your kids, friends, and family are valuable, so you pay attention to them. Do you pay attention to the value that God brings to your life? You must understand the magnitude, the great importance of God's love for you. When you know the value, true awakening to God's love that casts out fear happens. Here is my prayer for you as you process God's deep love and great character: "And may you have the power to understand, as all God's people should, how wide, how long, how high, and how deep his love is" for you (Eph. 3:18 NLT). That's depth. That's magnitude.

## Fear Is a Counterfeit Love

Now that we are settling into understanding the depth and magnitude of God's love, we need to understand a big point. Fear is a counterfeit love, and, if left unchecked, it can make you do some crazy things. Where fear is operating, love cannot freely flow. Failing to recognize that we are operating out of fear means losing our footing fast. Fear loves to mask itself as a concern. It says things like, *You better get that lump checked out. You know Grandma Joyce died of cancer, which will probably happen to you.* Sure, getting a lump checked out is wise, but do you see the trickery baked into that fear thought? There is a difference between concern and worry. Concern moves you to action, and worry stops the action. Concern says, *I have a genuine problem, and I need a plan to solve it.* Worry says, *I have a real problem, and the action I'm going to take is to be anxious.* Fear makes you feel like it cares by raising concerns, but it tricks you into believing untrue things. On the other hand, love cares and gives you solutions for your worries that calm anxiety and bring about peace.

We have already covered how much God loves you. Now that we understand that, let's look at what the Bible says about love conquering our fears. The fourth chapter of the book of 1 John contains a foundational scripture I lean on regularly. "There is no fear in love. But perfect love drives out fear, because fear has to do with punishment. The one who fears is not made perfect in love" (1 John 4:18 NIV). There is no better scripture to describe fear. In some versions, it says fear has to do with torment. In my opinion, there is nothing more tormenting than fear that causes panic and anxiety attacks.

## Types of Fear

There is a healthy fear. The fight-or-flight kind of fear protects you from danger and tells you not to jump into the deep end when you can't swim. When the hairs stand up on the back of your neck when you find yourself in a dangerous situation, you know you need to get out now. Protective fear is a suitable type of fear, and we need to thank God for it. We welcome and are grateful for it.

The fight-or-flight response is a beautiful gift from the Lord that needs to be activated on purpose when danger arises, not because our lifestyles are such that we are always running at supersonic jet speed.

Then there is fear of the Lord. Fearing the Lord is commanded in the Bible. One example is found in Proverbs 14:27 (NIV): "The fear of the LORD is a fountain of life, turning a person from the snares of death." Why would God ask his people to fear him when repeatedly he tells us not to fear? Fear, in this sense, is defined as awe or reverence. Fearing our heavenly Father means respecting, honoring, revering, and walking in wonder and delight before him. We should all have this healthy fear for our deep and great God.

The best way to fear God is to know his word by spending daily time in the Bible. A study by Barna Group in 2021 showed that only 16 percent of US adults read their Bibles regularly. Clearly, the benefits of knowing God's Word are undervalued in our world today. It's no wonder Americans are stressed out and anxious. We are unresponsive to the most important tool that can bring us peace. God's Word is not dead and dull. In fact, it is quite the opposite. "For the word of God is alive and active. Sharper than any double-edged sword, it penetrates even to dividing soul and spirit, joints and marrow; it judges the thoughts and attitudes of the heart" (Heb. 4:12 NIV). I want something sharper than a double-edged sword judging my thoughts and attitudes; I'm sure you do too! Our problem is that we don't know God's Word well enough for it to be able to protect us. Renewing our minds starts with knowing God's Word. Then, and only then, will we be able to recognize the voice of the enemy speaking lies to us. I created a chart that I often refer to when I'm trying to determine if the enemy or God is speaking to me.

# GOD'S VOICE
## VS.
# SATAN'S VOICE

| God's Voice Is | Satan's Voice Is |
|---|---|
| Peaceful (2 Thess. 3:16) | Stressful |
| Comforting (2 Cor. 1:4) | Depressing |
| Convicting (Rom. 8:1) | Condemning |
| Encouraging (Ps. 32:8) | Discouraging |
| Orderly (1 Cor. 14:33) | Confusing |
| Leading the Way (Isa. 40:11) | Forceful |
| Reassuring (2 Tim. 1:7) | Frightening |
| Calming (Ps. 46:10) | Rushing |

Let's get back to types of fear, one of which is unhealthy fear, and we should not allow it to run rampant. We experience harmful fear when we listen to Satan's voice instead of God's. Once you recognize it, you should stop it immediately. We will learn how to recognize and stop fear in Chapter Seven. Until we get to that chapter, it's important to note that we all experience fear differently, often in different ways during different seasons. In a recent season, I felt a heavy amount of unhealthy fear. I want to share a part of my journal.

Setback–Cancun—1.5.2022

My thoughts feel relentless. Torture. A constant poker trying to ignite fear. If I'm diligent in fighting the thoughts, the fire never takes off. It just sparks. When I'm not diligent, I let doubt in, and the fire of fear spreads. It starts with a simple whisper that seems like my thoughts but feels like darkness: "You are losing so much hair" or "Your swimming suit doesn't fit, you are gaining so much weight, something is wrong with you." Then, those thoughts planted caused me to think about all that could mean. Does everyone get interrogated by these types of thoughts, Lord? I feel alone with how this happens, and it affects me so deeply. How come my mind doesn't align with my heart and God's Word, which I know is true? Why do I struggle in this way, Lord? Is this my story forever?

Father, I need the tools, wisdom, strength, and stamina to fight this war. I feel worn out. My mind feels broken, like a missing connection is short-fused and keeps highlighting these evil thoughts repeatedly like a broken record. Suicide is not my story. But I have deep empathy and compassion for those who just want the torment to end. Father, I'm crying out for help. Please, teach me how to cope with hope. I want to flourish. I want freedom from this hell. I believe you can do it. I'm sorry for anything I have done to add to this fire. Jesus, forgive me. Help me overcome.

Did my vulnerability make you uncomfortable? David in Psalms laid out a vulnerable journal entry, too. Could our vulnerability with God be a vehicle he uses to heal us? Can we heal when we don't talk to God about our pain?

*I'm hurting*, Lord—will you forget me forever? How much longer, Lord? Will you look the other way when I'm in need? How much longer must I cling to this constant grief? I've endured this shaking of my soul. So how much longer will my enemy have the upper hand? Take a good look at me, Yahweh, my God, and answer me! Breathe your life into my spirit. Bring light to my eyes in this pitch-black darkness or I will sleep the sleep of death. Don't let my enemy proclaim, "I've prevailed over him." For all my adversaries will celebrate when I fall. I have always trusted in your kindness, *so answer me.* I will spin in a circle of joy when your salvation lifts me up. I will sing my song of joy to you, Yahweh, for in all of this you have strengthened my soul. My enemies say that I have no Savior, but I know that I have one in you! (Ps. 13:1–6 TPT)

We will all face unhealthy fear, worries, and anxiety in this lifetime. I am comforted that we can see examples of that in the Bible. We need to talk to God about our fears. He already knows them anyway. When we bring our worries to him, he can cover them with his love. The problem is not recognizing your anxieties; it's hiding them. My journal entry above discloses that fear is still a struggle for me, but that struggle is identified and brought to the feet of Jesus each time. The power of his word is sharper than a double-edged sword. It pierces through the scariest fear and the most severe anxiety. Now that we understand the depth and magnitude of God's love, let's learn how to stop the snowball of fear.

# CHAPTER 7

# Catch the Snowball

I once had a panic attack after my oldest son had heartburn. He decided to eat an entire buffalo chicken pizza in less than three minutes before rushing to get to youth group. He complained of chest pain later that night when he returned home. Because the Holy Spirit lives inside me, I immediately felt the peaceful reassurance that his chest pain was just heartburn. But instead of pursuing that peace, I let a negative thought invade my mind that sounded like, *What if his chest pain is a blockage in his artery and he has a heart attack?* With that negative thought, the snowball of more thoughts began to roll down the hill. As those thoughts gathered momentum, I became powerless as the snowball rolled over me. The result? Deep breathing and pacing in my bedroom while working through a panic attack.

"Jesus replied: 'Love the Lord your God with all your heart and with all your soul and with all your mind'" (Matt. 22:37 NIV).

I read this scripture and easily understand the calling set before me to love God with everything I have. But there is more to the story. Have you ever thought about what it looks like to love God with all your mind? God wants us to love him with our heart and soul, but he also wants us to love him with our mind. Have you thought about the distinction between the heart, soul, and mind? When you love someone, it's common to say, "I love you with all my heart and soul." But do you ever take it one step further and say, "I love you with all my mind"? You may be chuckling because that's not a typical saying in today's culture. Yet, saying *I love you with all my mind* simply means *I will love you in my thoughts and attention.* Our thoughts and attention need to be tuned in to God's love and promises if we are to love him with our whole mind. The goal is to align every thought with the heart of God. But what does that even mean?

Our thoughts have a lot to do with the anxiety that manifests. You can learn to control thoughts that snowball into anxiety by renewing your mind. Learning how to do this has been the most powerful tool I have found to help circumvent anxiety. I will teach you a five-step process to stop the anxiety snowball: recognize, replace, recite, repeat, and refuse. However, before we learn how to renew our minds, we must understand why there is a battle for our minds in the first place.

Do you realize there has been a strategic plan to destroy our trust and connection with God since the beginning of time? This plan is so cunning and crafty that you will question God's goodness and love for you if you buy into it. Genesis 3 reveals this plan to us. The serpent (*serpent* means "deceiver") is introduced, and it is our main opposition. His name is officially Satan, which means the great enemy of God's people. Friends, the battle is on. If you are a child of God, a follower of Jesus, you must not stick your head in the sand and ignore that we have an enemy seeking to steal, kill, and destroy, as described in John 10:10. Instead, you must have a solid and effective battle plan.

## A Stroll through the Garden

Let me take you back to the Garden of Eden, where a man and woman named Adam and Eve, created in the image of God, lived. This garden was perfect. God provided for their every need, and they had no worries in the world. They lived in paradise. God had one request: "You must not eat from the tree of the knowledge of good and evil, for when you eat from it you will certainly die" (Gen. 2:17 NIV). One day, the serpent made his way onto the scene and asked Eve, "Did God really say, 'You must not eat from any tree in the garden'?" (Gen. 3:1 NIV).

"Did God really say . . . ?" Wow! What a crafty question to get you thinking. Did you read that slowly enough to let the previous sentence sink in? I wrote "to get you thinking" because everything starts with a thought. Your thoughts can sink you or make you soar. Don't you want to soar? Don't you want to rise above any crafty ideas Satan sets up against the power of God? Unfortunately, as the story unfolds, Eve did not think the right thoughts. She took the bait of Satan, and she convinced her husband to feel the same way, too. From the same tree that God forbade them to eat fruit from, they ate the same fruit together, all because they believed a lie and listened to a thought that consisted of, "Did God really say?" Sin entered the world with their decision to eat the fruit. They engaged in the war the enemy has been trying to perfect since the beginning of time, a fight you have the power to overcome: the battle of the mind.

## Satan Tries with Jesus

The enemy may tempt you to fall for a bunch of lies, and he did the same to Jesus as well. There is a riveting story found in Matthew

4:1–11 that has opened my eyes to Satan's mind games. I want to take some time to dissect it deeply because I believe it has profound implications on the mental gymnastics that take place in our daily lives.

The story begins with Jesus fasting for forty days and nights. He was led into the wilderness to be tempted by Satan by enduring three specific tests. One was a test to break his God-ordained fast and turn some stones into tasty bread and eat. Next was an invitation from Satan to throw himself off a cliff and command angels to catch him. Third, Satan tempted Jesus to bow down and worship him in exchange for power.

Let's break down these three tests in today's lingo. First, when I'm hungry, people better watch out. I'm not bragging about this imperfection in my personality; I'm just being honest. You better not mess with me when I'm hungry because I get hangry. Therefore, how incredibly rude of Satan to approach Jesus while he had been fasting forty days and forty nights and tempt him to eat. Or was it rude? All along, Jesus knew what would happen. While many argue that Jesus was tempted when he was weakest, I say that, after forty days of fasting, he was the strongest—not physically, but spiritually.

The point of fasting is to take your eyes off this world and put them back on God. When the juicy smell of a Big Mac and perfectly split salty french fries floats your way after the first day of fasting, you better believe you're praying for strength to overcome that temptation. However, as time goes on, feeding your flesh becomes less important, and hearing from God becomes the priority. When you fast, you spend extra time praying and connecting with Jesus.

Satan led Jesus into the wilderness for temptation. I don't know about you, but when it comes to spending time in the wilderness, the last thing I want to do is fast from food, which often brings me so much comfort. But can I suggest something countercultural? Fasting drops us to our knees in prayer and allows us to connect with Jesus in a way our soul desperately needs. In those moments of focus and dedication to Jesus, we find answers, strength, and courage to fight whatever battle or temptation comes our way.

It might have been a low blow for Satan to tempt Jesus with bread right off the bat, but isn't that the point of an enemy? You know your opponent well when you go in ready to win a battle. In whatever battle you have shown up for, you have studied, planned, and prepared to win. It's no different with our adversary. Satan can't read your mind, but he is aware of your actions. Satan knew Jesus had been without food and water, so he went for the jugular right out of the gate. But a blockade immediately stopped Satan's blow. As a result of his close connection with his Father through fasting and prayer, Jesus was ready to win the battle of the mind. We would be prepared for more fights if fasting and prayer were a priority in our lives. To be brutally honest, I don't want to paint the picture that I am perfect in this area of spirituality. I need to take my own advice more often on fasting and prayer. I understand the importance, but usually, I lack determination. Thankfully, there is no condemnation in Christ. Also, it is important to note that fasting is not a command but is more of an expectation. If Jesus did it, then I will obediently fast, too.

After Satan tried to get Jesus to turn stones into bread, something brilliant happened. Jesus boldly proclaimed Scripture back to Satan on how important it is not to live on bread alone but on every word that comes from God's mouth. The physical needs of our life are not as important as our spiritual needs. Round 1 went to Jesus!

Round 2 started with an exciting rumble with Satan trying to get Jesus to throw himself off a cliff and then ask God to swoop in and save him. To me, the most interesting part of this passage is that Satan quoted scriptures found in Psalm 91:11–12 to get Jesus to sin. Read this loud and clear: Satan knows Scripture. The question is, does he know it better than you do? To avoid being fooled by his clever schemes, you must know God's Word. Study Scripture carefully and in context to understand God's principles for living. Knowing Scripture well, Jesus fired back a firm and quick response that let Satan realize it is not right to put God to the test. Round 2 went to Jesus!

Next, Satan tried something flashy. He couldn't get Jesus to eat or throw himself off a cliff, so he needed to pull out all the stops in an attempt to appeal to Jesus's pride. Scripture depicts Satan taking Jesus to a mountaintop that overlooked all the kingdoms of the world and their glory. "'I will give it all to you,' he said, 'if you will kneel down and worship me'" (Matt. 4:9 NLT). What Jesus said next is a total knockout. "Get out of here, Satan. . . . For the Scriptures say, 'You must worship the LORD your God and serve only him'" (Matt. 4:10 NLT).

I have so many questions after studying these passages. Did Jesus raise his voice at Satan or just speak calmly and confidently? What was Jesus thinking when Satan was talking bogus stuff to him? During Jesus's encounter with Satan, did he hesitate, or did he realize that Satan was feeding him lies right away? Lies are so dangerous, and Satan is the father of all lies, according to John 8:44. A quote by Joseph Goebbels, a Nazi propagandist, sends chills through my bones: "If you tell a big enough lie and tell it frequently enough, it will be believed." We must know the truth to combat lies. Satan threw big lies at Jesus, but he denied them and won the third round. Then, the devil went away, and angels came and cared for Jesus.

Don't you want the devil to leave you alone, too? Don't you want to win the battlefield of the mind? It won't come easy, but it will come if you prepare for battle. So how do you get prepared? I'm glad you asked! Let's dig in.

## It All Starts with a Thought

In the book *Who Switched Off My Brain?*, Caroline Leaf says, "Thoughts are measurable and occupy mental 'real estate.' Thoughts are active; they grow and change. Thoughts influence every decision, word, action, and physical reaction we make. Every time you have a thought, it is actively changing your brain and your body—for better or for worse."[1] Our thoughts matter. We have healthy thoughts and toxic thoughts, as Leaf further explains. We will reap the consequences if we don't learn to immediately recognize toxic thoughts.

Understanding how God made our brains is incredible. Science is catching up with Scripture. It is possible to prove what God tells us in Scripture with science, and I enjoy learning about that. Although the science is important, this chapter barely scratches the surface. If you desire to dig deeper into how your thoughts and body are connected, I recommend following Caroline Leaf. She has blogs, books, and podcasts chock-full of helpful resources. My goal in this chapter is to explain my success with recognizing toxic thoughts and learning how to rewire my brain so it is not as susceptible to toxic ways of thinking. When I diligently rewire, I fall prey to anxiety attacks far less. The Bible calls this "renewing your mind" (Rom. 12:2).

## The Bible and Toxic Thoughts

Three scriptures have changed my life for the better when it comes to renewing my mind and fighting anxiety. First is Romans 12:2: "Do not conform to the pattern of this world, but be transformed by the renewing of your mind. Then you will be able to test and approve what God's will is—his good, pleasing and perfect will" (NIV). This scripture indicates that we have the power to transform by renewing our minds. Things don't have to stay the same way they have always been. That's good news! We do not have to conform to the world's way of thinking and living. God's ways are higher, different, better. I have made it a priority in my life not to follow the practices of the world but of God. It is worthwhile to follow his ways, even if they go against the prevailing current. The second part of the scripture is just as powerful. It says we will then know what God's will for our life is. Do you see the correlation? Think right, get right. In the power of right thinking lies our purpose in life. Positive thinking is not the same as renewing your mind; right thinking is rooted in knowing and meditating on God's promises.

Second Corinthians 10:5 is a life-changing scripture for me because it teaches us to demolish any thought or idea that makes us doubt or think against God. The scripture also calls us to stand up and fight against lousy thinking or ideology so negative thoughts do not snowball out of control. The war for our minds is on like Donkey Kong. The apostle Paul, in 2 Corinthians 10:3–5, set out a clear directive using military terminology. We are at war; God must be first in charge—we must surrender our lives to his will and control. As followers of Jesus, we can't be lazy with our thoughts. We must seize every thought and fight to make it line up with God's Word.

The exposure to memes, books, celebrities, social influencers, movies, TikTok videos, ideas, and thoughts that lead to wrong ideas and desires are many, but you have a choice. You can recognize the danger and turn away, or you can allow unhealthy thoughts to take you captive and swallow you up. You capture bad ideas, and you honestly admit them to the Lord and ask him to redirect your thoughts. Our focus cannot just be whatever we want it to be. We must dismantle any arguments, claims, or ideas that set themselves up against God.

A third life-changing scripture regarding renewing our minds is Philippians 4:8: "Finally, brothers and sisters, whatever is true, whatever is noble, whatever is right, whatever is pure, whatever is lovely, whatever is admirable—if anything is excellent or praise-worthy—think about such things" (NIV). I can see where this scripture can breed a power of positivity mind-set. The importance of thinking positively is true. The Bible tells us so. But we can't just think positively and forget to be vulnerable with God. Sometimes, positive mind-sets can be harmful because they don't allow us to be authentic. We can recognize our negative feelings and still choose to make positive choices with our emotions. Speaking of recognizing, that is the first step in renewing our minds.

## The Five Rs

Now that we have a firm foundation on what Scripture says about renewing our minds, let's learn how to do it. The first step is to recognize, which requires getting real with yourself. I regularly do a thought dump in my journal; I write out my authentic feelings and emotions. When I'm in a healthy rhythm, thought dumps get done at least once a week. I do them when I feel bothered, anxious, fearful, depressed, stressed, or confused. Realize that you cannot overcome something you have not acknowledged. The effort of writing your thoughts out is a critical step. In a thought dump, you write down all the things bothering you. Don't hold back. Sometimes you may even think to yourself, *There is no way I can write this down. I don't want anyone to know I'm thinking these things.* Do it anyway. Write it out. The light of God's love can't shine on the dark thoughts you believe if they remain hidden in your mind. I will take you through one of my thought dumps first before we tackle yours. It's easier to recognize and take action on someone else's negative thoughts than your own. Take a deep breath, and let's work through this together.

## Christy's Thought Dump

*I don't hear God's voice right.*

*I make too many mistakes.*

*I feel like a failure—a terrible leader, mother, friend, and wife.*

*I care too much about what people think of me.*

*No one holds people to biblical truth anymore.*

*I feel like I'm the only one. It's lonely.*

*Everyone is against me.*

*I don't have what I need to accomplish what I'm supposed to do.*

*There are so many unknowns. That scares me.*

We need to recognize the themes of these negative thoughts before they snowball out of control. Doing a regular thought dump is vital for that reason. If you're having a bad negative-thought day, I recommend that you do a thought dump immediately. Negative thoughts sneak in when you least expect them. It's important to be wise and ready with your battle plan when negative thoughts attack you.

The next step is to sift through each thought carefully. I will warn you that this is time-consuming, but please remember, anything worthwhile is always worth some time and effort. Once we recognize the theme or subject matter of the negative thought, we will move on to Step 2, which is replace. But first, let's examine one of my thoughts: *I don't hear God's voice right.* To understand that thought further, we must turn to the ultimate source of truth: the Bible. What does God's Word say about hearing his voice? Every time we dissect and recognize a negative thought, we must ask ourselves, what does God's Word say about _____ (you fill in the blank)? For my first example, the question is: What does God's Word say about hearing God's voice?

There is an excellent tool called a concordance in the back of most Bibles. It lists words that show up in the Bible, and it sometimes even has a subject index. In the back of my Bible, the New Living Translation Parallel Study Bible, I looked up the word *voice*. It listed several scriptures, including John 10:3, which reads: "The gatekeeper opens the gate for him, and the sheep recognize his voice and come to him. He calls his own sheep by name and leads them out." Because I was not exactly sure what that scripture meant, I went to the commentary portion of the Bible and read for further explanation. I discovered this scripture explains that Jesus is the good shepherd. God's people represent his sheep. When we spend time with Jesus like shepherds spend time with their sheep, we recognize his voice. In context, this scripture is saying that we hear God's voice. What a beautiful promise! The negative thought, *I don't hear God's voice right,* is a bald-faced lie from Satan. I hear God's voice, I now recognize that negative thought as a lie, and I will no longer give in to it.

Let's try another one from my thought dump: *I care too much about what people think of me.* I usually don't recommend Google searching when it comes to health concerns, but for finding truth in God's Word, Google can be a helpful tool. So, let's ask the question we must ask whenever we deal with negative thoughts. What does God's Word say about people pleasing?

OpenBible.info has a list of sixty-seven verses that address people pleasing. I read over them, and the one that resonated with me the most was, "For am I now seeking the approval of man, or of God? Or am I trying to please man? If I were still trying to please man, I would not be a servant of Christ" (Gal. 1:10 ESV). This scripture is boldly helping me recognize that I cannot be a servant of Christ and please man at the same time. To overcome people pleasing, I must understand what God's Word says about not doing it. When I know that I only need to please God, it takes the pressure off me to be all things to all people, and it brings freedom to my soul.

Now it's your turn. If you have never done this before, you may have hundreds of negative thoughts to dump. Let it rip! Maybe you don't have hundreds of negative thoughts but have several nagging ones that replay on repeat in your mind. Get those out. Don't overthink this exercise. There are no right or wrong answers. Start dumping now. When you have completed your thought dump, pick the top three negative thoughts you want freedom from, and recognize what the lie or theme of the negative thought is. Remember, you do this by asking yourself the question: What does God's Word say about_____?

The next step is to replace. It's easy to fulfill this step after recognizing the theme or lie. Here is what you do: Write down your negative thoughts again, and then scratch them out and put the new truth you just found from God's Word right underneath it. Take some time to rewrite the replacement in your own words. Let me show you how this works:

> *I don't hear God's voice right.*
> God's Word says that his sheep hear his voice (John 10:3).
> Therefore, I won't believe the lie that I don't hear God's voice.
>
> *I care too much about what people think of me.*
> God's Word says that I cannot be a servant of Christ and please man simultaneously (Gal. 1:10). I will stop pleasing people and focus only on pleasing God.

We can't just recognize negative thoughts. We must take it a step further and replace them. Take a moment to rewrite your top three negative thoughts/lies, and replace them with the truth found in God's Word.

The devil can't read your mind, but he can react based on your actions. That is why the next step is so important. Recite: "Death and life are in the power of the tongue, and those who love it will eat its fruits" (Prov. 18:21 ESV). The power of the tongue goes both ways. We can speak negatively or positively—God's Word or Satan's lies. Our words contain both death and life. We must recite truths out loud for Satan to hear. If Jesus did it, then why are we not doing the same?

Reciting truths out loud does several things. It puts Satan in his place because reciting makes a bold statement of where your loyalty lies, which is with God. When Jesus stood firm on truth, Satan left Jesus alone (Matt. 4:11). I'm not saying that once we recite, we will never hear from Satan again. But what I am saying is that life is full of individual battles we must win. Each time we stand firm on God's truth, we win one of those battles. Reciting also rewires your brain. When we choose to meditate on praiseworthy and excellent thoughts filled with God's truth, we rewire those neuropathways damaged by toxic negative thinking.

Step 4 is repeat. Repetition makes renewing your mind easier over time. When you repeat the five Rs, eventually, over time, it will become second nature to you. Consider the route you take to work or a familiar grocery store. Do you think about how to get there? You have repeated the drive so many times that you could finish it while your mind was entirely focused on something else. That is what I want for you with the five Rs. You have repeated the steps so often that negative thoughts are recognized instantly and replaced automatically, and there is a loud recitation of the truth.

Loud recitation leads me to the last step, which is to refuse. Your mind is a muscle, and it takes work to be strengthened and renewed. You must be ruthless and refuse to give up. Walking through thought dumps often brings up painful emotions and deep negative thoughts. It is normal to need help when working through a thought dump. If you need help working through your mess, this is a great time to pick up the phone and call a Christian counselor. Don't try and tackle painful and damaging thoughts all on your own. I also speak thought dumps to my inner circle (which I will explain more about in Chapter Eight). They often help me recognize and replace the lies with God's truth when I'm having difficulty seeing it for myself. You may also find it beneficial to run your thought dump by a pastor or other trusted godly leader in your life. Regardless, refusing to give up is the most important step of this process, and the company you keep plays a massive part in helping you refuse not to give up. Let's explore that more, shall we?

---

NOTE

[1] Caroline Leaf, *Who Switched Off My Brain?* (Nashville: Thomas Nelson Publishers, 2009).

# CHAPTER 8

# The Company You Keep

It was 2020, and I was on a boat in the middle of the Gulf of Mexico and experiencing deep sea fishing for the first time in my life. The company was good; I was with my husband and four dearest friends. In no time at all, I was reeling in my first big catch, an Atlantic bonito. The laughter and cheering by my friends and husband elevated my already high adrenaline rush. As my fish made it onto the boat, I did a celebration dance. There were lots of pictures and laughter. Out of nowhere, my joy turned into spewing. Yes, you read that right: spewing. Without my permission, the sea had made me sick. While I was getting sick, my husband could barely keep me from falling overboard. My vision went double, and my balance became questionable. Being in the middle of the ocean, throwing up, seeing double, and not being able to stand straight is a recipe for disaster when you struggle with anxiety. Vacations can be triggers for me anyway, since my nervous breakdown began on one. Not wanting to destroy the rest of my friends' fishing excursion, I prayed for help. Unfortunately, Jesus didn't heal my seasickness, and I got worse by the minute. Now, not only was I seasick, but I was also battling a panic attack! The captain decided to call a rescue boat for me, which was an answer to my prayer. My friend Sarah wasn't too fond of the deep sea fishing experience either and happily jumped onto the rescue boat with me to get to dry land. Again, I wanted my friends and husband to enjoy all the benefits of the fishing trip, so I encouraged my husband to stay. Sarah and I sailed away in the middle of the Gulf of Mexico on a rickety rescue boat with two men who didn't speak English. Let's just say that added to my anxiety. I breathed deeply, fought intense nausea, and prayed we would sail to dry land quickly.

Thankfully, I felt comfort in my body when I put my feet on steady sand, but my mind was still getting tossed by the waves of negative thoughts. My thoughts screamed, *You can't control this panic attack. Do you know what happens when a panic attack starts? Another one is coming. Your equilibrium is off now, and you will feel sick forever. You are going to land yourself a stay in a Mexican hospital.*

I told Sarah I needed to walk. She found a comfy seat and kept an eye on me as I walked. I often fight panic-driven thoughts with a prayer walk. As I paced the beach, I battled more and more intrusive negative thoughts that wouldn't let up. I was already weak and tired from getting sick on the boat, and I didn't have a lot of energy to fight the mental battle going on either. It was the moment of truth. Would I tell my good friend what was really going on? At that point, I had not told anyone I was in the middle of a panic attack. I could have easily hidden behind the seasickness, and no one would have ever known. From the outside, I appeared to be doing fine; I wasn't throwing up anymore, but what was happening inside me was far from fine. At that point in our friendship, Sarah had only known about my past panic, but I had never invited her into my present panic. Our friendship experience so far gave me no reason to believe she would judge me if I let her in, but even so, it's hard to be vulnerable. I took a calculated risk. I broke down.

"Sarah, I'm not doing okay. My mind is racing. I don't think I'm struggling with seasickness anymore but rather with a panic attack. Can you pray for me?"

She looked at me with so much care and compassion, and she jumped on the opportunity. As people passed us on the beach, she covered me in mighty prayer. As tears rolled down my face, I knew our friendship had moved into a new category.

## Help Others Love You

When you struggle with anxiety, you need to realize that not everyone can handle you. I have found that most of the people I interact with genuinely don't understand the torment I deal with when panic and anxiety bubble to the surface. But I learned that people can love you well even if they don't know what you are experiencing. When I realized that I needed love, not just understanding, it changed how I accepted help from my friends and family.

Later in this chapter, we will cover categories of people I have in my life. Once I have explained the types, I will describe who I believe are the safest people with whom to share your anxiety struggles. But first, we must learn how to identify our feelings of anxiety and communicate what we need with those safe people. People can't help you if you just say, "I'm anxious today." We need to know ourselves well enough to understand why we feel anxious. Once we have identified the why, then we can advocate for ourselves properly. Advocating for yourself takes some work, but I have the tools to help. Dwain, one of my wise Christian counselors, gave me several questions I should ask myself when I feel anxiety coming on:

- What specifically is the problem?
- What part of this can I control?
- What part of this can I not control?
- Is this a problem I can solve? If so, do I want to?
- If I can solve the problem and want to, what am I going to do next?

Let's use my example of seasickness to walk through these questions. What specifically was the problem? I was on a boat that was making me seasick. What part of that could I control? I couldn't control the waves of the sea that were making me sick, but I could control getting off the boat. I was too worried about upsetting my friends' excursion, so I didn't ask soon enough for a rescue boat. How many times do we do that in our own lives? We suffer through something because we are worried about upsetting someone else, which costs us something in return. Don't do that. Learn to walk through these questions right away, and don't be afraid to be bold and ask for what you need. Speaking up for yourself is not mean; it's wise.

I couldn't prevent the seasickness or how long the rescue boat would take to come. I also couldn't control my friends' responses. Thankfully, they were compassionate, and my friend Sarah felt horrible about what I was experiencing. But even if she had not acted that caring, her response was her responsibility. You don't have to hide your hardships to make someone else happy.

Next, could I solve the problem I was facing, and if so, did I want to? Of course, in that situation, I wanted to solve the problem because I was miserable. The solution needed to come as soon as possible. However, there are situations, such as in parenting or leadership, for example, in which you may have a problem arise, but you don't want to jump in to solve it because you want the people you are leading to be able to think for themselves and learn a lesson. In those situations, *What am I going to do next?* is an important question. A good solution would be to surrender the problem to God and let him work it out. I realize that surrender is not easy, so we will learn how to sincerely surrender in Chapter Eleven. But it's important to note that not every problem is ours to solve. Sometimes, doing what Exodus 14:14 says is the best way to handle a problem causing anxiety: "The LORD will fight for you; you need only to be still" (NIV).

If there is a problem for you to solve, doing something about it matters. Too many people know what's causing their anxiety, yet they make zero effort to make a change. Don't live in the cycle of crazy by doing the same thing every day and expecting change. Don't stay in the rut of a friend that keeps gossiping about you, a dysfunctional relationship that you keep protecting, an unhealthy work environment that is causing you to compromise your morals, the friend circle you hang with pushing you further away from God, or even the smoke alarms that we talked about in Chapter Five. Ignoring these things and expecting them to just magically get better is foolish and will only snowball into even more anxiety. The most extensive advice I can give you in overcoming fear and anxiety is to TAA—take action always. My action step in the seasick example was to get off the boat and tell my friend Sarah I was battling anxiety and racing thoughts, and I needed prayer.

Let's recap. When fear and anxiety hit and you need support, it's vital to communicate with your loved ones about what's going on. First, identify what the problem is. Work through the rest of the questions until you get to the last one, which should lead you to an action step. Then you will be ready to communicate to your loved ones what you need.

It's your turn. You can use these questions to identify the cause of your anxiety and how to stop it. Now, pause to reflect, pray, and journal your answers:

- What specifically is the problem?
- What part of this can I control?
- What part of this can I not control?
- Is this a problem I can solve? If so, do I want to?
- If I can and want to solve the problem, what am I going to do next?

In Chapter Two, I talked about my boss, who allowed me time off during my nervous breakdown. He was very gracious to me. You may be thinking, *I'm not that fortunate.* If you have a boss who is not understanding and would never allow you to take off if you had panic attacks, I want to help you with something: your pause is your priority. If you need to take time off, then the only thing stopping you from doing that is you. I hear you fighting back right now, saying, *That's not true; if I take time off work, I'll get fired, which will lead to no paycheck, which will lead to not being able to pay my bills.* Is that the case, or have you just worked up the worst-case scenario in your head? Often, we don't take care of ourselves because we project what we think someone will say or do to us if we are honest with them about our condition. There are times when the person we need to be understanding just isn't, and there are consequences to us missing whatever we have committed to but can't fulfill, like a shift or shifts at work. That's when we must make big decisions. If we have gotten to the point of having constant panic attacks that disrupt our lives, is it worth it to keep pushing through? The answer is always no. We must be diligent about what is creating the panic and anxiety, and we must communicate what we need to whomever needs to hear it. We may disappoint some people in that process, but taking care of our health should always be a top priority.

## Anxiety Is Not a Badge of Honor

We can't use anxiety as a cop-out, either. Telling someone what you need may cause fair disappointment in whoever was counting on you if you must bow out. You need to own that and apologize for letting your people down. You can't hide behind your anxiety as an excuse to not perform, and you should not wear anxiety like a badge of honor. On the flip side, you must not power through like a superhero, because powering through will eventually leave you powerless, like in my case. There is a delicate balance between telling people what you need and owning how your anxiety has affected someone else.

One time my husband and I got invited to a fancy, all-expenses-paid trip with some good friends. I asked the friend who invited us who else would be traveling with us. He began to list off a bunch of people I did not know. I instantly knew this would be a trigger for me. Old Christy would have just gone on the vacation, and then when anxiety flared up, I would flash my anxiety badge and run away to get out of the fun and to be alone. That behavior makes things awkward. I have done it many times. I'm not saying that anxiety won't flare up, and you will need to leave from time to time. That happens to the best of us, and there is grace in those rare occasions, but you shouldn't have a perpetual pattern of flashing your anxiety badge to get out of whatever you are doing. The lesson? Vacations needed to be enjoyed with my safe people during this stage of my life. Now that I know my anxiety boundary, it's easy to stick with it. Here is the million-dollar question: How do you know who your safe people are?

## Categories of People

Knowing what type of person you are dealing with is essential when you decide to open up to someone about your mental battles. Just because someone is family doesn't automatically mean they are safe to share with either. Even lifelong friends are not always the safest people.

Your inner circle is the first category of people. These are the people who have your back. They never get sick of your pain. They unconditionally love you, fight for you in prayer, and check on you frequently. With these people, you are not afraid to be real. You can speak unfiltered with them, and your darkest, innermost thoughts get expressed. They hold you accountable, and you hold them accountable. They would do anything for you, and you would do anything for them. It's a two-way relationship, not a one-way street. They know you better than anyone else, and they are running the same race as you. You share a deep connection that overlaps with your passion and purpose. There is only room for about three to five of these people in my life because it's too difficult to maintain that level of intimacy with more. If you're part of a married couple, your spouse should be part of your inner circle.

Next is your pouring category. I believe you should constantly be pouring out to someone and that someone should be pouring into you. These are your mentors and mentees. You do life with them in a way that helps them grow, and they are helping you grow. These are precious relationships that connect at a deep heart level, but they are not as close as your inner circle. These relationships are often sought out and don't just fall into your lap.

The next category is your close family and friends. These people love you but don't necessarily get to know everything about you. They are the people you may go with to events, church, small groups, and parties, and you may see them during the holidays, but they are not necessarily people you check in with daily. There is a deep love and mutual admiration in this category of people, yet there is a level of intimacy that is just not crossed. You keep your conversations simple and focused on the happenings around you and the events you attend together. Occasionally, you may share a problem you are working through, but you keep the details at a minimum and are cautious about how much you share.

People in your work relationships category are people you must do life with every day since it's where you earn a paycheck. Sometimes these people can become other categories of friends, but mostly they are just casual friends you see every day and whom you interact with because you have to. You share the same work goals, which will often help you grow in connection, but if you had to move from that job, you probably would not see these people again.

Those in the convenience category are people whom you cross paths with regularly because you are neighbors, share a carpool, or your kids and their kids interact regularly. They make your life easier, and you make their life easier because you share the burdens of working together to get daily life tasks accomplished. There isn't a deep connection, just mutual respect to help each other out.

Your acquaintance category includes people you see regularly but don't engage with more than a smile or high five. You probably see these people at the gym, the grocery store, your kids' school, or the church lobby, or maybe you drive by them daily in the parking lot. You know their name (possibly), but you don't know their story.

In the authority category are pastors, counselors, doctors, and leaders. They speak into your life in a specific area. They have wisdom that you don't have, wisdom that is needed to live a healthy life.

## To Share or Not to Share

The safest category of people for you to share your mental health battles with is your inner circle. Beth Moore's brilliant saying has helped me frame to whom I open up: "Be authentic with all. Transparent with most. Intimate with some."[1]

Let's start with "intimate with some." Jesus did this so well. Not everyone went to the mountaintop with him, and not everyone in your life gets the privilege of going to the mountaintop with you. Peter, James, and John were in Jesus's inner circle. They had a remarkable experience with him, as recorded in Luke, Mark, and Matthew. I could give you the gist of this experience, but I think it would rob you of imperative inner circle lessons. So instead, let's read together the account found in Matthew 17:1–9 (NLT). Note: I'm going to interject my thoughts on inner circle prerequisites along the way. The Bible has great wisdom to help us with relationship anxiety.

**"Six days later Jesus took Peter and the two brothers, James and John, and led them up a high mountain to be alone."** The first point from this passage is that high places are reserved for high people—the inner circle. My inner circle has a nickname: eagles. Why? Because eagles are known for flying at high altitudes; it's how they soar so beautifully. If you want to soar in life, you must learn how to fly high. Chickens and ravens peck and poke, but eagles soar high and rise above the insignificant things in life. The next point from this passage is that you need to spend time alone with your inner circle. In this day and age, there are so many social media exchanges. Everyone is accessible, and anyone can start a "friendship" with you. I believe social media interactions create a false sense of intimacy. Authentic inner circle relationships are formed by spending real, quality one-on-one time together.

**"As the men watched, Jesus' appearance was transformed so that his face shone like the sun, and his clothes became as**

white as light. **Suddenly, Moses and Elijah appeared and began talking with Jesus.**" Within your inner circle, you experience things together that no one else sees, and no one else will understand but your inner circle.

"**Peter exclaimed, 'Lord, it's wonderful for us to be here! If you want, I'll make three shelters as memorials—one for you, one for Moses, and one for Elijah.'**" When God has blessed you with an inner circle, you recognize it's a privilege to be a part of it. You don't take it for granted, and you often celebrate what God has done in and through your relationship. You often stop to remember big moments by making memorials of things that have happened. All that means is that you do something special to remember what God has done in your life. My friend Sarah calls these "God lights." A framed photo, jewelry, or souvenir is a perfect "memorial," as the scripture says to remember and celebrate the wins. On a recent trip, our eagles' circle got bracelets that say "soar" to help remind us of the gift God gave us through our friendship.

"**But even as he spoke, a bright cloud overshadowed them, and a voice from the cloud said, 'This is my dearly loved Son, who brings me great joy. Listen to him.'**" Inner circle people understand how important it is to listen to the voice of God. Your relationship is bonded and formed stronger by seeking him in all the plans you have together. Inner circle people hear the voice of God on their own and have a personal, intimate relationship with him, which makes your relationship with them stronger.

"**The disciples were terrified and fell face down on the ground. Then Jesus came over and touched them. 'Get up,' he said. 'Don't be afraid.' And when they looked up, Moses and Elijah were gone, and they saw only Jesus.**" Inner circle relationships equip and encourage you to overcome fear by pointing you back to Jesus. They realize that fear and anxiety are a normal part of life, so they have compassion for you when you fall, but they always help you get back up.

**"As they went back down the mountain, Jesus commanded them, 'Don't tell anyone what you have seen until the Son of Man has been raised from the dead.'"** You uphold a level of confidentiality within an inner circle that you wouldn't dare dream of destroying. Keeping things private allows you to feel safe, and the peace that comes with maintaining confidential things feels like a high level of protection.

You may be thinking you don't have anyone to add to your inner circle who meets those prerequisites. My best advice to you comes from an extraordinary leader, pastor, and best-selling author, John Maxwell. He gave a message on the characteristics of eagles and said, "Eagles attract other eagles." What does that mean? If you want an eagle in your inner circle, first become one. Then, pray for other eagles to fly into your life.

Another safe place to share your anxiety burdens at an intimate level is with the authority category. Because of the nature of their position, these people are generally trustworthy. They are bound to a level of integrity due to their profession. I understand that isn't always the case; there are definitely bad pastors, doctors, counselors, and leaders, but for the most part, sharing with someone in the authority category is a safe move. Do your homework first. Check around and see their track record and reviews before jumping into an authority relationship with them. As soon as you have identified the problem, it will take some wisdom on your part to know which authority you should contact. If your concern is spiritual in nature, then a pastor is a wise decision. For example, if you have a hard time understanding a principle found in God's Word or need advice on how to walk through a conflict from a biblical viewpoint, ask a pastor. If you have deep-rooted reoccurring fears and anxieties, beginning a relationship with a Christian counselor is smart. Going to a doctor when smoke alarms are present and not going away is also a wise move. Through my journey with anxiety, I have found that I often see people from more than one authority category at the same time; there is nothing wrong with that.

## Transparent with Most

Transparency works excellently with the pouring, work, close friends, and family categories. When I think of transparency, I think of a glass shower door. Often, it's frosted glass. You can see through it, but you can't see everything. That's how you should be with most people. Be honest and share stories, but you don't need to share everything. Just like you wouldn't open your door during a shower to just anyone, don't open your heart to just anyone either. I have confused transparency with intimacy too often, and it has burned me. Transparency is filtered, and intimacy is unfiltered. Choose wisely with whom you share.

The real you, your authentic self, is the person God made you to be. Don't hide your personality, talents, strengths, and weaknesses. Being authentic means not denying that you are having a bad day, but you don't have to give all the juicy details either. You can speak openly about your struggles with a mindset that doing so may help someone else. Authenticity means accepting the way God created you and not trying to change it. I am not talking about unhealthy behaviors or sin. Those need to be corrected and repented. I'm talking about your God-given personality, the beautiful qualities that make you you. Never act one way with people from one category and act differently with people from another category. That's the opposite of authenticity. That's called fake. Be the same in public as you are in private. When you achieve that, then you are walking in genuine authenticity.

After identifying safe people to share with, how do you communicate how you need to be loved and supported within your inner circle? Generally, I need three main things when experiencing anxiety: space, comfort, and truth.

For the most part, when I feel anxious, I need some space and time to get my head right. Warning: some people will use space as an excuse to isolate themselves for days or weeks. That is not healthy and is not what I'm talking about when I say space. Being alone for a small amount of time is very helpful. Nourishing space for me makes room for praying, worshiping, journaling, and asking why I feel anxious or fearful. Space also helps us to not be codependent. When you're scared, being alone might be the last thing you want to do, but I want to challenge you to run to Jesus before running to anyone else. People cannot solve our fears and anxiety—only God can.

After taking some space, I let my inner circle know what would comfort me the most by sharing with them what has triggered me or is causing anxiety. Speaking it out is very powerful; I almost immediately feel relief. I let my inner circle know I need prayer. Generally, by this point, being alone has served its purpose, and it isn't good for me to continue to be alone. So I will ask someone to join me for dinner or come over to my house for a walk. Sometimes anxiety puts me behind on housework. Real inner circle friends will help you out with whatever you need. Sometimes that looks like a meal, picking up groceries, or doing a few loads of laundry. Asking for that type of help has not always been easy for me to do, but speaking up for myself on what I need has proven extremely helpful when anxiety flares. What comforts you? Your people can't read your mind, so it's important to let them know what will bring you relief.

Last, I need the truth spoken to me. You want your inner circle to comfort you *and* be truthful. God's Word is the truth that needs to be said to us, even if it's hard to hear. If I have stepped off the path and am doing something that is creating anxiety in my life, they will call me out on it. Believe me—you want that accountability in your life. Sometimes, I'm not doing anything wrong, and I just need to be reminded of God's Word so it can bring peace to my situation. Inner circle people are truth speakers. Welcome it. It's a gift from God.

The most important lesson of this chapter is "bad company corrupts good character" (1 Cor. 15:33 NLT). The company you keep plays a pivotal role in overcoming fear and anxiety. Who will you pull close when it matters?

---

NOTE

[1] Beth Moore, *Sacred Secrets* (Nashville: LifeWay Press, 2013).

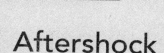

# CHAPTER 9

# Aftershock

On August 7, 2021, I was at the farm preparing for a weekend with friends to watch IF: Lead when I decided to check in on my father-in-law, Mike, who I nicknamed Papa B. Mike had an appointment with his oncologist that day, and I believed that he would receive good news. His fight with cancer typically responded well to chemotherapy, and I had no reason to think this round would be any different.

"Hey Papa B, how are you doing? How did the appointment go?" There was a long pause, and I could tell he was emotional.

"Christy, the doctor told me to stop chemotherapy because it wasn't working. I would be lucky to make it to Thanksgiving. I knew that was probably hard news for him to deliver, so I made sure to tell him I appreciated him and that he was a good doctor to me."

A flood of thoughts and emotions came over me. I wondered how he would tell this heartbreaking news to my husband and our children. I thought about the words Papa B had just told me and how they couldn't be true, that it was just a bad dream. Simultaneously, I also thought what an extraordinary man he was. In his greatest time of need, he chose to think of someone else over himself by encouraging the oncologist.

He proceeded to talk. By this time, he was so emotional I could barely understand him. "Christy, I love you. I sure am glad Troy found you. You are a great disciple of the Lord."

Any shred of calm in my voice was gone. With tears gushing, I said, "I love you so much. We are going to get through this."

After getting off the phone, I was full of sadness, and I threw the phone across the lawn overlooking our small lake. I didn't want to face this truth set before me, yet I didn't have a choice. Thankfully, my dear friend Katie, who was there for a girls' weekend, heard the conversation and was immediately by my side, and we wept together.

Papa B's announcement marked a significant setback of anxiety for me. I often call anxiety setbacks aftershocks. After an earthquake, it is common for aftershocks of varying sizes and durations to happen. My major earthquake was the nervous breakdown, and since then, I have been more susceptible to anxiety and panic. A heat stroke victim is also more vulnerable to a reoccurrence once it has happened. It is no different for me with anxiety. Learning to ride the waves of fear is crucial in not letting the waves take me down. My epicenter is anxiety over death and disease for someone I love or myself. After Papa B's call, the fear that has always haunted me became a reality.

## Troubles of This Life

In this life, we will have trouble. Jesus himself makes sure to remind us of that in John 16:33. Trouble often shows up and brings anxiety along too. Sometimes these troubles are brought on by our poor choices, and sometimes it's just the way life goes because we live in a fallen world. When anxiety is caused by our own doing, we must get honest with ourselves and take inventory of our difficulties because anxiety stirred up by sin never leads to peace. When my pastor gives messages that cause us to be self-reflective, he calls them "crowd reduction messages." This part of the chapter could be considered a book sales reduction message. Stay with me; it may be challenging, but it's definitely worth it. Here is a short list of questions I will often ask myself when troubles come, to help me determine if I have done something to initiate my anxiety:

- Have I been disobedient to God?
- Am I holding a grudge or walking in unforgiveness?
- Am I distant from God?

Have I been disobedient to God? The Bible is the road map to life. In it, we find how to live. You may be thinking: *Sure, Christy, it's a large book with lots to read. How do I know if I'm being obedient to God or not?* Only you and God can determine your obedience. But to find victory over fear, we must submit to God, and obedience tests our submission. His Word is a package deal; surrender to him means submission to the Bible. We can't honor God with obedience without pursuing the Bible. All throughout the Bible are practical ways to remain obedient to God. A scripture I found that speaks loudly to this idea is 2 Timothy 3:1–7, which lists some major things that could call us to disobedience, such as arrogance, obsession with self, unholiness, and lack of self-control, just to name a few. I don't want to pick a fight, but you may be guilty of some of those things right now, too. But guess what? You are not alone. I still struggle daily with many on the list, and thinking more highly of myself is at the top. It's hard to kick the super-woman tendencies, you know? The root of that is being too proud. Let's take a look at the full list of disobedience triggers:

- Lover of self
- Lover of money
- Proud
- Arrogant
- Abusive
- Disobedient to parents
- Ungrateful
- Unholy
- Heartless
- Unappeasable
- Slanderous
- Without self-control
- Brutal
- Not loving good
- Treacherous
- Reckless
- Swollen with conceit
- Lovers of pleasure rather than lovers of God
- Having the appearance of godliness, but denying its power

Do you struggle with any of the items on this list? We don't want to have a log in our eye and judge the speck in someone else's. We need to take an honest look at anxiety levels. Could you be adding to the problem with your unholy behavior? Take some time to journal or circle the bullets that seem to be a problem for you. I trust you are being honest with yourself. With that honesty, can you now see why this could contribute to rising anxiety levels? It's essential to investigate, especially if you want to walk in freedom. Use time in prayer and in God's Word, church, and godly community to take inventory of the anxiety you are experiencing that you may be causing.

Am I holding a grudge or walking in unforgiveness? In my experience, anytime I have chosen to be bitter, hold a grudge, or purposefully stay mad at someone and walk in unforgiveness, the consequence is always anxiety. Unforgiveness locks you inside an isolated, restless prison. God's Word is evident in this. Jesus said, "But when you are praying, first forgive anyone you are holding a grudge against, so that your Father in heaven will forgive your sins, too" (Mark 11:25 NLT). It's too costly to hold a grudge. Why? If we want God to forgive us, then we must forgive others.

I want to be clear on what forgiveness is not. Forgiveness does not diminish hurt or pain or give someone permission to keep abusing you. It is the acknowledgment of a wrong. Forgiveness takes strength from God to do. Trust that he can turn your pain around for good and his glory.

Please understand that we cannot forgive what we do not acknowledge. Once I learned about forgiveness in the Bible, I had difficulties for a while, but probably not how you would think. I wanted God to quickly forgive me of my sins, so I jumped quickly to forgive when people sinned against me. It seems like the correct thing to do, right? But I wasn't finding freedom from forgiveness. I still felt locked in a prison of pain and anxiety. It wasn't until I saw a Christian counselor who taught me that part of forgiveness is acknowledgment. We can repeatedly say, "I forgive you," but if we don't truly take time and space to process the hurt and pain we have encountered by someone else's sin, our forgiveness will likely not be genuine; it will be lip service at best. Take time to acknowledge your pain with God.

Here's a last important tip on forgiveness: extending forgiveness is not dependent on the other person apologizing. With or without an apology, we must forgive. I hope I didn't give you more anxiety—I know this is tough. When dealing with people who have wounded you, it is wise to seek a Christian counselor if you have a hard time forgiving or need advice on moving forward. I walked through the steps of forgiveness and reconciliation with a professional counselor; without it, I would not be where I am today.

Am I distant from God? God's Word says in James 4:8, "Draw near to God, and he will draw near to you" (csb). Sometimes I think we want the peace of God without the presence of God. Peace and presence go together. I often find myself anxious when I am distant from God. If I ignore my Bible and forsake my godly community, I will live in stress. Making God our priority is key to overcoming the aftershocks of panic and anxiety.

## Fallen World

You have asked yourself the three questions and have determined you are right with God to the best of your knowledge. You are winning in obedience to God. You have forgiven those who have wronged you, and you are drawing close to God, yet you are still experiencing turmoil. Understand this: just because trouble comes doesn't mean you caused the trouble. The effects of Adam and Eve, the fall of man, and Adam and Eve's deliberate choice to disobey God brought pain and suffering into our world. Because of their poor decisions, we now pay the price. Facing trials is a common theme throughout the Bible, and those trials often happen when you feel like you have been faithful. Being a Christian does not exempt you from trials; it equips you for them. We have an enemy whose number one job is killing, stealing, and destroying (John 10:10). He wants to defame the name of Jesus and destroy your relationship with him. As a Christian, you have a target on your back. It's not if trials come, it's when trials come, but there is always hope!

Walking through the end of Papa B's life was an unbearably hard trial. We watched him decline rapidly. A man who was always on the go became bedridden. As the end approached, he struggled to breathe, moaned in pain, and seemed detached from reality. These words may be triggering some anxiety. I want to be mindful of that because I understand. Yet, I want to teach you an important lesson: fear is worse than the trial itself.

God's grace is in the trial, but God isn't in fear. After this trial, I can confidently say that fear is tormenting, and trials are laced with God's grace. Yes, dealing with the loss of Papa B was unbearably hard, but it was also beautiful. We watched God show up time after time through loving community, meaningful conversations, and straight-up peace that surpasses all understanding.

One of Papa B's desires was to build a lake that our family could enjoy. He pushed the project through quickly and got it dug. A lake doesn't fill up overnight. Typically, it takes many months to fill, and it could even take years. Before he lost the ability to walk, a neighbor across the road drained his lake for repairs and filled ours up. The sunset over the new lake was stunning. It was such a joy to our family to see this lake filled. I believe God was filling us with a beautiful gift, too—the gift of grace. God's grace fills us when we are in our darkest moments. His grace enables strength, courage, and power to face anything we must endure, even death. I wrote this in my journal shortly before Jesus took Papa B home on October 31, 2021:

> On the top of a skyscraper, you can see the world differently than the way you see it from the ground. This difficult season is forcing me to see things from a higher perspective. If our family weren't facing this hardship, would we have spent this much time together? Or instead, would we have filled our schedules with more of what doesn't matter? Would we have spent this much time talking, learning, and looking through memories, or would we have instead stared at screens and ignored

each other's presence? Would we have prayed this hard for strength, or would we have instead leaned on ourselves, a counterfeit to real power? Would we be asking the hard questions to God that build our faith, or would we instead have continued living life on autopilot like we are gods? Would we have talked about how heaven is real, or would we instead have continued to act like this world is our home? This difficult season has strengthened my faith.

I'm learning that my faith doesn't exempt me from trials; it equips me for them. That's the skyscraper perspective you often can't see from the ground.

With a skyscraper perspective intact, there was more to endure. Troy lost his grandma less than two weeks later. Process this with me: My mother-in-law lost her husband, and before she could even catch her breath, she lost her mom, too. Grueling grief and pain swept through our family. I don't know who came up with this, but it has been said that death comes in threes. A dear friend, Beth, also lost her precious husband in that same timeframe. We hadn't even thrown away the tissues from Papa B's funeral before we went to two more. Once that was all over, we settled in at home to adjust to our new normal. Days later, Troy, my middle son Landon, and I tested positive for COVID-19. When we needed our friends and family the most, we instead got isolation and sickness. Don't get me wrong, our friends and family were remarkable during that time; it's just not the same when you must grieve in quarantine. The kicker was, it was my fortieth birthday too. Not how you want to ring in the big 4-0!

Within the ministry I ran, I was also wrestling with some uncharted waters in leadership. Threats and abuse from within began to circulate, and it crushed my already mangled heart. For four straight months, I had endured constant waves of anxiety. Think about being in deep waters for that long. Because of your circumstances, you can't return to dry land for rest and strength because outside forces keep pushing you back into the deep. An aftershock was on the way, and I had an aftershock—a rather large one.

I sat down at my computer in my home office to lead a Zoom meeting for work, and I couldn't catch my breath. *Is this COVID or panic?* I managed to collect my thoughts and lead the meeting, but I no longer had a distraction from my out-of-control thoughts after it was over. I didn't practice the five Rs, and the small snowball that started with *Is this COVID or panic?* built major momentum as I recalled all the horror stories I heard about people dying from COVID-19. It didn't take long before I couldn't breathe. My heart was beating out of my chest, and I felt weak in my knees. I had a panic attack.

Since I have dedicated my life to helping people overcome panic and anxiety, it is hard to admit when I have aftershocks. I always think to myself, *Christy, you know better than this; don't let your thoughts snowball; stop the panic before it stops you.* Sometimes it's just not that easy. Life is hard, fears are real, and sometimes panic and anxiety win. Below are three things I have learned to embrace when an aftershock hits.

## Aftershock Tips

*Tip 1: Don't try to hide it. Sometimes you just need to say, "I'm having a panic attack." Denial adds more weight to your already heavy chest. Remind yourself of the symptoms you had during previous panic attacks so your mind doesn't try to feed you with lies that something else is wrong with you. It has been a tremendous help to have my panic attacks journaled to go back and recount what I went through. The beast of panic makes you think that old symptoms are new ones. An even more significant aftershock could be waiting for you when that happens.*

*Tip 2: Be kind to yourself. Shaming yourself into believing you are weak, faithless, and worthless only perpetuates the anxiety cycle. Give yourself some space to breathe, rest, and relax, because aftershocks don't last forever. Taking inventory of where you are and what triggered the aftershock is wise. Fools ignore aftershocks; wisdom excavates them to find out what's under the surface. A big trigger is exhaustion—more on that in just a bit.*

*Tip 3: The aftermath can leave a mess. When your body has a panic attack, it can take awhile to rebound. Just like an aftershock hitting an area leaves a crumbly mess, so does panic in our bodies. I used to wonder why I felt off days after a panic attack, but now I know it's normal for my body to need time to rebound after an aftershock, which helps bring me peace. I'm careful to avoid extra stress in the days following an aftershock, and I often make sure to get extra rest and exercise. A good clean diet helps as well. Unhealthy foods loaded with carbs and sugar add to the already crumbly mess.*

## Power of the Pause

Our world celebrates busyness in unhealthy ways. We don't rest and take time to be still like we should. In fact, stillness is rarely even practiced. Quick question: How often do you take time to pause in God's presence? I suspect it's not that often. What if you did? How would that change your life? This stat further confirms my point of busyness: 14 percent of US adults have tried meditation. First of all, that's not a lot of people. Fourteen percent is low. Even though that's low and shows that most Americans don't slow down very well, meditation doesn't always mean stillness with God. Often people will try and quiet their minds with no desire to connect with God. I see this as a dangerous road that leads to self-help. We should never be alone with our thoughts without God. In Psalm 46:10, a beautiful expectation is before us: "Be still, and know that I am God" (NIV). The calling is to "know" that God is God, that he is large and in charge. In stillness, we learn to surrender, to acknowledge our worries and cares and give them to him. We rest and ponder the vastness and wonder of God. It's a time to delight and cherish his deep love for us. Stillness brings us peace because we proclaim his power over our lives.

In the quiet, we switch our focus to Jesus, where we find rest and rejuvenation to attack the day with courage. Being still isn't just a good idea; it's a weekly command that God asks us to do.

> Remember the Sabbath day by keeping it holy. Six
> days you shall labor and do all your work, but the sev-
> enth day is a sabbath to the LORD your God. On it you
> shall not do any work. . . . For in six days the LORD
> made the heavens and the earth, the sea, and all that
> is in them, but he rested on the seventh day. Therefore
> the LORD blessed the Sabbath day and made it holy.
> (Exod. 20:8–11 NIV)

If we can't give one full day to God, are we trusting him to be God? Although this book is not about how to practice stillness with God, I pray that you understand how important it is to pause and why the Bible tells us to do so. As mentioned, exhaustion can be a massive trigger for me with anxiety. When I'm not diligent about stillness with God, I get depleted quickly.

John Mark Comer has written an excellent book called *The Ruthless Elimination of Hurry*. I have read it three times. In the book, Comer beautifully explains why hurry and busyness are destroying our lives. He teaches how to connect with God in a way that makes sense and is practical. I hope you learn to meditate, a daily pause to focus on Jesus in complete stillness. As I mentioned earlier in this book, your pause is your priority. No one can hit the pause button for you. It's yours to protect. It's yours to put in motion. Someone can try to force you to pause, and people in my life have strongly encouraged me to do so in the past, but unless the power of the pause is given priority in your walk with the Lord, you won't pause. You will power through. And powering through will leave you powerless. When you can be alone with the Father, you can regain strength, which gives you lifegiving energy.

When I was first diagnosed with severe panic and anxiety disorder, I had aftershocks regularly. Now, my aftershocks are few and far between. I believe that can be your story too. Don't try and hide them, be kind to yourself, and remember that aftershocks take time to rebound from. When the aftershocks do come and shake you, don't lose hope. Instead, take heart because Jesus has overcome the world, and he is ready and willing to help you clean up the crumbly mess.

# CHAPTER 10

# In This Life, You Will Have Trouble

Have you ever received a text from someone that stops you dead in your tracks? Something so meaningful and full of power that you think about it for days and it changes how you look at life? That happened to me in January 2022. My dear friend, Will, texted me:

> There is a beautiful scene in The Matrix where Morpheus tells Neo some of the rules in the Matrix can be bent, and others can be broken. Morpheus has faith that Neo can be fast enough to break those rules. Neo asks, sarcastically, "So what are you telling me? That I can dodge bullets?" To which Morpheus replies, "No. I'm telling you, that when you're ready, you won't have to."
>
> I have an impression of this scene for you. Neo becomes fast enough to dodge bullets. Later, he matures enough to

*stop them. As you believe in Jesus more and more, your faith will increase. You will receive more abilities to slow down every entry point of fear and deception. You are empowered to examine them. To submit them to God. To overcome. To stop them. I am praying and believing this over you, my dear friend!*

Friend, you made it this far through the book; I believe you want to stop the fear bullets instead of just dodging them! The truth is, we won't live a fearless life, but we can learn to live more fearlessly. In other words, we won't be totally fearless, but in time, through building our faith, we will learn to fear less. In this life, we will have trouble bullets that fly at us in the form of fears, worries, and anxieties, but the absolute good news is fear surrendered to Jesus brings us peace. I hope you're learning how to understand anxiety, smoke alarms, and further acceptance of God's love for you. My prayer is that you can begin to take control over the spiritual battle in your mind, talk more openly with the people you love about your anxiety, and face your anxiety aftershocks with courage. None of this is easy to do, but I believe the Lord will guide you in each of these steps.

This life is not easy, and, unfortunately, we will have trouble come our way. The truth of the matter is that we are at war against the dark forces of this world. "For our struggle is not against flesh and blood, but against the rulers, against the authorities, against the powers of this dark world and against the spiritual forces of evil in the heavenly realms" (Eph. 6:12 NIV). Once we become Christians, there is a target on our backs. Satan releases his dark forces every day, and we are tempted to turn from God and walk in sin. These forces are real, but we must not be afraid. When we belong to Christ, the victory is ours. The good news is that God did not leave us powerless. Engage and win the war by putting on the whole armor of God. I'm a visual learner, so I'm supplying an image that will help you absorb the full armor of God (Eph. 6:10–18).

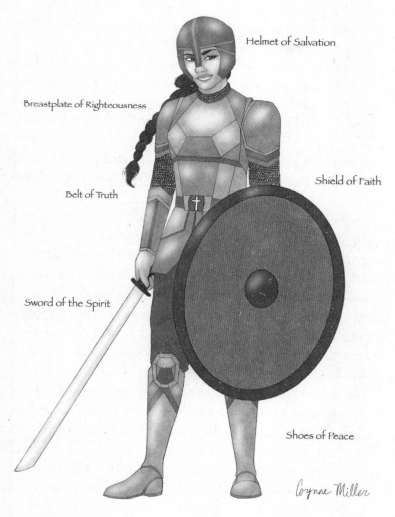

Helmet of Salvation

Breastplate of Righteousness

Shield of Faith

Belt of Truth

Sword of the Spirit

Shoes of Peace

*Lynne Miller*

Every piece of God's armor is crucial if you want to stand firm against the enemy's plans, especially if you're going to fight and win the war against fear and anxiety. You need to suit up every day.

I realize this may be a foreign concept to you, so if you want to study the armor of God in more detail, I highly recommend you purchase Priscilla Shirer's Bible study *The Armor of God*. For now, I will give you a short snapshot of each piece of armor and why I think it's essential to circumvent fear and anxiety.

*The belt of truth.* A great belt holds an entire outfit together. The belt of truth is the Word of God, and it keeps our life together. God's Word should be the core of our being, and we cannot be successful without it. When we don't know God's Word, we are powerless against fear and anxiety. His Word is our faithful armor and protection against every fear we face. We buy insurance policies to protect items of value. God's Word is our insurance policy for life.

*The breastplate of righteousness.* A breastplate protects our vital organs, like the heart and lungs. Righteousness is the act of being morally right and just. When we turn from sin and obey God, we wear the breastplate of righteousness, which helps protect us from what sin destroys. We should not underestimate the power of sin to destroy. God detests sin, and there are consequences for our sins. It's crucial to address sin quickly; we leave our vital organs open for attack when we don't. The outcome of that is always anxiety.

*The shoes of peace.* These shoes are not just ordinary shoes. The apostle Paul describes shoes the Roman soldiers wore that were laced with metal spikes that did two things. They helped the soldiers keep their footing in rugged terrain, and they provided protection when an enemy attacked. Can you imagine getting kicked in the hamstring by a shoe with metal spikes? Yikes! One of the most significant tactics of the enemy is to get you to lose your footing with Jesus by creating chaos and a lack of peace in your life. Not lacing up our shoes of peace daily means we are not ready. Do you go to the store without shoes? No, you sure don't.

A sign that you are prepared to go is that you have shoes on. It's no different with the shoes of peace. When we put them on, we are prepared for battle, ready to share the gospel, and walk in the peace of God, not the spirit of fear.

*The shield of faith* isn't wimpy. The types of shields Roman soldiers used were the size of their entire bodies. Imagine holding up a door over your body when fiery darts get thrown at you. That's how those shields looked. Our faith covers us like a big door. When fears come rushing in, we need immense faith as protection to stop the incoming assault.

*The helmet of salvation.* The Roman helmet provided insanely good coverage. There was only a space for the soldier's eyes. The goal of this helmet was to protect the head and neck thoroughly. We all know that if our brain is damaged, it affects our entire body. The same is true for the mind and soul. If our minds are damaged, our souls will be too. The helmet of salvation is crucial. Jesus died for our sins so we could have eternal life. When we become saved, we are not wholly sanctified. Our life is a journey to look more and more like Jesus every day. Our choices reflect our salvation. Are we making choices that show Christ's likeness within us? We are to "work out [our] salvation with fear and trembling" (Phil. 2:12 NIV). "Fear and trembling" does not mean we should be afraid of losing our salvation. We should instead be in awe of the gift of salvation that we have been given, and we should have a deep reverence for the opportunity to represent Jesus. Winning the war of the mind and overcoming fear and anxiety requires us to put on the helmet of salvation daily.

*The sword of the Spirit.* I think of my Bible as a sword to get this word picture correct. Every time I speak the Word of God over my fears and anxieties, I'm stabbing the enemy. Scripture tells us that "the word of God is alive and active" and is "sharper than any double-edged sword" (Heb. 4:12 NIV).

*The last weapon is prayer.* Prayer helps us deal with worry and should be an active and continual part of our life. We gravely underestimate the power of prayer. Prayer also helps us deal with fear. Process this powerful scripture: "Don't worry about anything; instead, *pray* about everything. Tell God what you need, and thank him for all he has done. Then you will experience God's peace, which exceeds anything we can understand. His peace will guard your hearts and minds as you live in Christ Jesus" (Phil. 4:6–7 NLT—emphasis mine). In my opinion, prayer is the most potent weapon we have in our arsenal.

With the further understanding that we are at war and have a complete set of armor, I want to ask you a question inspired by my friend Will. Are you dodging fear bullets, are you stopping them, or are you being destroyed by them? Take a moment to answer that question honestly. Are you dodging, stopping, or being destroyed by the enemy's bullets? Let me explain the differences between the three.

## Dodging, Stopping, or Being Destroyed

Dodging means you are tired. You keep jumping up and down, squatting and rolling all around to dodge the fear bullet when you could just activate the armor of God to stop them completely. Now, there are days when you have some victories over fear and anxiety. For example, you don't let your thoughts snowball because you have recognized their entry, and you do a pretty good job of stopping fear thoughts the moment they arrive on the scene in your brain. Because you have your belt of truth on, you use your sword to cut through the garbage the enemy feeds you. You also do a pretty good job of extinguishing the enemy's fiery darts because you have your shield of faith activated. But if you are honest, most days fear bullets still get through because you are using your own strength to dodge bullets, and you feel worn out.

Stopping fear bullets means you wear your armor faithfully, and the second a fearful fiery shot gets launched, you immediately recognize that fear is not from God. Therefore, activate your full armor of God with your shield of faith lifted high, yell "access denied," and the fiery bullet gets extinguished with no damage to you. You stand firm and walk triumphantly in the shoes of peace daily.

Being destroyed means you don't have your helmet of salvation on, and you get knocked out by the enemy's fear bullets frequently because you are in the war without the proper protection. You are getting hammered by fear. If this is you, there is no condemnation in Christ Jesus. Cry out to God for help. Repent and turn to him. Put on the armor of God, and refuse to go into battle unprotected.

I can honestly say I have a deep desire to stop fear bullets and not dodge them anymore. I believe the encouraging text my friend Will sent me that says, "As you believe in Jesus more and more, your faith will continue to increase. You will receive more abilities to slow down every entry point of fear and deception. You are empowered to examine them. To submit them to God. To overcome. To stop them. I am praying and believing this over you, my dear friend!"

I believe it for you too, my friend. By the power of Jesus, you can stop fear in its tracks and live free from anxiety. Let me note that freedom doesn't mean there won't be occasional aftershocks. I believe you can still be walking in freedom if you have a setback. It's what happens in that setback that defines your freedom. Did you learn from it, and did you bounce back quickly? We all get knocked down from time to time.

Now, here is some news you might not want to hear. "The testing of [our] faith produces perseverance" (James 1:3 NIV) in our life. By going through challenging situations, we grow and build our faith. Fear is a necessary blessing that helps us develop our faith. If there were never anything that challenged our faith, how would it grow? In Chapter Nine, I reflected on the trauma our family experienced in 2021, and I lamented the loss and how much anxiety I experienced. My husband told me, "Christy, have some grace with yourself and look at all you have been through in this season. Can you see how far you have come and how much your faith has grown?"

Troy was right. There is no way I would have bounced back from three deaths, our family getting COVID, and leadership struggles without great faith. That great faith developed over time by overcoming obstacles. Each time an obstacle came, it was an opportunity to learn, grow, and build my faith in Jesus.

The problem is that we want the easy button to work in everything we do. In our modernized information society, help and resources are all at the click of a button, which makes things easy. Faith doesn't come with an easy button. Earlier, I mentioned John 16:33, and it deserves repeating. Here is what Jesus said: "I have told you these things, so that in me you may have peace. In this world you will have trouble. But take heart! I have overcome the world" (John 16:33 NIV). "Take heart" is such a key phrase; it means to be bold and courageous and to take your thoughts captive. You will face difficulties in life, but we are assured peace and joy in Jesus, not in the world, when we are bold and courageous in the face of hardship and suffering. We are never alone because we have the most victorious power, Jesus, on our side.

# CHAPTER 11

# Wave the White Flag

I boarded a ski lift ride called the Chondola that would take my family up the Smoky Mountains for spectacular sightseeing and incredible family fun. Our feet dangled as the single bar came over our heads to protect us from falling out of the seat. My youngest daughter seemed like she could easily slip through the space where the seat and the bar came together. I looked up, and there was an iron piece that clasped the seat to a steely rope that pulled us up the mountain. Then, fear set in. The thoughts came rushing in. *What if the rope breaks? What if that iron clasp comes detached and we fall to our death?* I white-knuckled that safety bar the whole way up the mountain as if it could save me, and I barely took time to breathe. I had no control over my circumstances, and I panicked. More fear rose with every inch we climbed.

That's how our world is, too. Unless we are grounded in the firm foundation of Jesus, we wind up striving for something that's not godly. We try to make it to the top of something, and with every inch we climb, fear rises. Globally, the pandemic of fear and anxiety is at all-time highs. I'm willing to put my neck out on the line and say something bold. Fear is rising because faith is dying. The need for control has us white-knuckling something, and it isn't God. We are not living our lives surrendered fully. God is often our last resort instead of our first response. Lack of surrender is how we open the door for fear and anxiety to take root.

Here is what I know for sure. Surrender cannot be partial—it must be complete. God wants our total surrender, not partial surrender. So, how do we become sincerely surrendered people of God, laying down our control and handing it to God? By the end of this chapter, you will better understand whether you are walking partially or fully in surrender and what to do about it.

Here is my definition: true surrender yields to who is in authority. It puts aside your agenda and elevates the plan of the one in authority. Our ultimate authority is the one and only Jesus Christ. True surrender asks daily, *What do you want me to do, Lord?* We continually seek his direction in the Word and in prayer; we genuinely want what he wants for our lives.

Are you yielded to the authority of Jesus Christ? How do you know if you are struggling with surrender? See if any of these statements ring true for your life:

- I think I can change people.
- I worry more often than I'm at peace.
- I like to hover over people and make sure they are doing things to my expectations.
- I have a hard time being in the passenger seat.
- I have confidence in myself but not in others.

- I trust myself more than I trust God.
- I often tell people how things will go and leave no room for other options.
- I rarely consult God.
- I compare myself to other people.
- I question the validity of God's Word.
- I would rather do things myself than ask God for help.
- I don't think God has my best interest at heart.
- I control my children because I don't want them to make mistakes.
- I don't want God's will in my life; I would rather do things my way.
- I'm confused about my purpose in life.
- I feel like my plan is the most important.

If you selected even one of these statements as something you struggle with, you might wrestle with being fully surrendered to God. Surrender is a daily choice, and it's not an easy choice. There are many people who will make it to heaven because they accepted Jesus as their Lord and Savior but are walking around feeling stressed out, anxious, and fearful because they have never learned how to surrender fully.

Salvation is not surrendering. Salvation is a decision; surrender is an ongoing choice. We make choices daily that are not rooted in surrender, like white-knuckling our circumstances. As I looked up at the iron piece holding my family suspended over the mountains, I had a choice. Would I or wouldn't I trust God? As I processed that choice, I began to think about how crazy it is that we hop on a Chondola ride and trust something manmade over God who made it all. Most people don't think twice about getting on a roller coaster, driving a car, being a passenger on an airplane, or taking a ski lift up a mountain. These are all manufactured items, and a lot of trust must go into the people who construct and operate these things for us to feel safe. If I could trust the iron piece holding my family on the steely rope to get us up the mountain safely, can't I trust God's hands even more in every situation of my life? Control is the opposite of surrender—lack of surrender stunts our faith. We don't want stunted faith; we want strong faith. This chapter aims to give you tangible tools to help you surrender each day to Jesus.

## Steps to Surrender

The first step toward complete surrender is to commit. Have you given your life to Jesus as Lord? If you need to review whether you are a fan or follower of Jesus, please go back to Chapter Three. A simple prayer at the end of the chapter helps lead you through the decision to commit your life to the Lord.

The next step to surrender is to commit to building your faith. "And it is impossible to please God without faith. Anyone who wants to come to him must believe that God exists and that he rewards those who sincerely seek him" (Heb. 11:6 NLT). When you don't have faith in God, how can you surrender? It's simple: you don't. Surrender is impossible without faith. Below are five practices that have impacted the growth of my faith the most.

One, get into the Word of God. We have a special plant in the cabin at our farm from the loss of my father-in-law. Our family skipped watering it for almost two months. Unfortunately, the plant looked extremely floppy and weak. I watered it and opened the curtains so it could get some sunlight. Within one day, it bounced back and was looking healthy again. The Word of God is the living water and light you need to survive. We need it daily to thrive and be strong. I can tell a big difference mentally, physically, and emotionally when I am not watering myself with God's Word. What I'm about to suggest might seem so elementary, but do you have a Bible? Are you reading it? Does it make sense to you? If you don't have a Bible, stop everything you're doing right now and buy one. I use several Bibles, but my favorite one is called the NLT Parallel Study Bible, TuTone. It has many commentary applications I can use to help me understand more clearly what I'm learning.

Second is prayer. While growing up, I thought prayer was a repetitious, religious act that you did to make God happy. Once I truly surrendered my life to Jesus in a meaningful relationship with him, I realized prayer was just a conversation with God. God yearns for connection with you just like your family and friends do. Prayer builds intimacy, trust, and relationship with God, and it reminds us daily that we are not in control and that he is. Prayer grounds us and centers us in surrender. When I started practicing prayer by journaling, I began to see God's faithfulness in a new way. When prayers got answered, it built my faith. Have some fun with this. Put a dry-erase board in an area of your home that you call your prayer space, and write down your prayers. When he answers them, celebrate. Or buy a prayer journal—they make cute ones that help you track your prayers and reflections. Journaling is a beautiful way to build connections and trust with God. It's fun to go back and look at old journals and see how far your faith has come.

Third, get connected to a body of believers. First, I want to explain the difference between the universal church and the local church. If you recall my story of finding Jesus, going to a local church did not mean I had genuine faith in Jesus Christ. Being a part of a church does not save you. The decision to follow and surrender to Jesus and repent from your sins does. When I committed to Jesus, I became a part of the universal church. The church, which Jesus is head over, comprises believers. The universal church is not a building or a particular denomination. Ephesians 1:22–23 says,

"And God placed all things under his feet and appointed him to be head over everything for the church, which is his body, the fullness of him who fills everything in every way" (NIV). This scripture means we are the church of Jesus Christ.

The local church is what has been given to us to grow in the knowledge of God. In addition, we are called to use the gifts that he has given us to disciple others. No more excuses—find a local church that teaches the Bible and bolsters your faith. Make church attendance a priority. Without community, we cannot live in a world overflowing with anxiety. Without community, our chances of overcoming fear and anxiety are bleak. God's people are your people.

Piggybacking off community, you also need godly friendships. Pursue people whose faith is greater than yours. Review Chapter Eight, "The Company You Keep," for a refresher. Also, encourage those whose faith is smaller than your own. Invite people to church. The Great Commission says to go make disciples (Matt. 28:19–20). We cannot do that without opening our mouths and sharing the good news of Jesus to everyone we know. Share how he has changed your life; your testimony is the most excellent witness to your faith.

The last way to build your faith is to pursue healing. Nothing will keep you stagnant in faith longer than bitterness and unforgiveness. I want you to know that I'm sorry for the hurt you have experienced. You didn't deserve it. Your pain is legit, and it's time to seek healing. I want to see your heart whole again. God wants us to pursue healing and not stay stuck in our pain. Bitterness rots the bones, and forgiveness sets you free. Don't delay any longer. Seek counseling for the pain you are experiencing.

You can't learn to surrender to God without building your faith, and I gave you five action steps to start that process:

- Commit to the Word
- Commit to prayer
- Commit to a local church
- Commit to godly friendships
- Commit to pursuing healing

The next step in learning how to surrender is to commit your actions to the Lord. Proverbs 16:3 says, "Commit your actions to the LORD, and your plans will succeed" (NLT). The scripture does not say to commit your actions to yourself, and then your plans will succeed. Yet we live committed to our plans every day. Why? Because we think we know better than God does how our life should go. Here is what I think happens, because I do it quite frequently. We play tug-of-war with God. *I got this, God. No, wait— you got it. No, wait—I got it. No, wait—you got it!* Here is a practical example: *God, you can deal with the parenting part of my life. But when it comes to money, I don't need your help because I've got it all figured out. I don't need you to help me out with my finances. But come to think of it, if you want to deal with my annoying boss, I will let you help me out in that situation.* Do you see how this works? We give parts of our life to God and then try to control the other facets. So often, we take over and make a mess of what God would have done best if we just stepped back and let him lead. Partial obedience is still a lack of obedience.

## My Story of Surrender

In 2011 I was aware of God but had no desire or care about surrendering my life to him. I was doing just fine without him. Do you know what that is? Pride. I was fully confident in my abilities. After all, I was a rocking sales manager and was incredibly successful at just twenty-nine years old. Why did I need to surrender? Pride is a perilous trap. God's Word has lots to say about the danger of pride, but the book of James says it the best, in my opinion. "God opposes the proud but gives grace to the humble" (James 4:6 ESV). "Opposes" is strong language. God opposes your prideful ways. He is not in support of you living your life independently of him. All our actions need to be committed to him because he cares about them. I have asked God what I should wear for a speaking engagement, what I should cook for dinner, and where our family should take vacations. If we get in the habit of asking him about our small actions, how much more will we rely on him for the big actions?

One time, my middle son Landon came to me and asked what electives he should take for middle school. My instinct was to tell him to just sign up for what he enjoyed most. Then I remembered the verse, "Commit your actions to the LORD, and your plans will succeed." I asked him if he had prayed about it yet. The answer was no, so we prayed about it together. During our prayer, I felt the elective I thought he was supposed to take come to my heart. God did the same for him. Sure enough, we both had the same elective come to us. The strange part was this elective was not his first, second, or even third choice. Yet, he signed up for it anyway. I believe my son's decision to take an elective that he was not excited about taking was a simple act of surrender. It's important to remember that surrender doesn't always make sense. Surrender also means it might not be your first choice. The world's narrative that says *Do whatever makes you happy* is not biblical. God would oppose a decision that fulfills only our fleshly desires. The humble route Landon chose was a decision infused with God's grace. It's far better to make a decision wrapped in God's grace than to make a decision that God will oppose.

The next step in surrender is to commit to discipline. Discipline is the practice of training people to obey rules or a code of behavior and using punishment to correct disobedience. This life is a training ground to become more and more like Jesus every day.

The fancy word for that is called *sanctification*, and being sanctified requires discipline. The Bible's commandments are the written
rules and code of behavior we should follow when we commit to
Jesus. When you understand God's deep love for you, the outcome
is a deep relationship with Jesus. Being in a deep connection with
Jesus leads to wanting to be obedient and following the rules. God
is indeed full of grace and mercy, but there are consequences for
not following the rules. Therefore, it makes sense that surrender
would take discipline and why it's something our world struggles
with so much. In Matthew 16:24–25, Jesus said to his disciples, "If
any of you wants to be my follower, you must give up your own
way, take up your cross and follow me. If you try to hang on to
your life, you will lose it. But if you give up your life for my sake,
you will save it" (NLT). We must take up our cross of surrender
and lay down our selfish ways. That takes discipline. The problem
is that the world tells us otherwise. Do you recognize any of these
worldly sayings?

- "Just do it."
- "Have It Your Way."
- "Because You're Worth It."
- "For everything else, there's MasterCard."
- "A Diamond Is Forever."

Everything these sayings promote is the opposite of what Jesus
promotes. These slogans advocate only thinking about your
desires. There is nothing wrong with lovely things and caring for
yourself. Please don't misunderstand me. But when it's rooted in
selfishness, it is wrong. The world's ways are not God's ways, and
that's why it makes it so hard to surrender. To follow God's way,
we must discipline ourselves to ignore the world's way.

The following helpful step in surrender is to commit to giving
up control. My recovery journey from the nervous breakdown

was very hard, with major ups and downs. I had completely given my life over to the Lord in surrender through the breakdown. Things were going quite well when out of nowhere, a pesky panic attack occurred. I went to my bedroom to pray. I felt a prompting during the prayer: *Give up control.* It took me several months to figure out what the heck that meant. I thought I had given up control. I was taking all the action steps to build my faith. I was putting God first (for the most part), attending church weekly, seeking the Lord regularly, reading his Word, and praying. But he wanted more, and I finally figured it out. He wanted me to quit my medical sales career. I was in total shock. The idea of quitting my successful career sounded crazy to me. My conversation with God sounded like this: *I can't do that, God; I have my master's in health-care administration. I spent a lot of money on the right education for this career. Surely you don't want me just to walk away from it? Plus, I have worked in my role for a long time, and I have earned it. I deserve it. And we need the money. I can't be a stay-at-home mom—I'll go nuts. I love my children, but you gifted me in sales. God, you have this wrong. Surely you don't want me to quit my job.*

I battled with God by using those excuses for a long time. I concluded that he was not going to change his mind. I heard and saw messages about letting go of control everywhere I went. The prompting never let up. It only got stronger. So, I decided to tell my husband. That didn't go so hot. He also thought the idea was crazy, and I didn't blame him. On a budget spreadsheet, that would be a foolish decision. Yet deep down, I knew God was calling me to end my sales career.

I began to pray that God would show my husband too. I knew I couldn't make this giant leap of faith without his love and support. A few days after that prayer, I got the idea to read *The Purpose Driven Life* by Rick Warren. I asked Troy if he wanted to read it with me. He agreed, and we decided to read it before bed each night. The book is set up for you to read a chapter a day for forty days. Something beautiful happened at around Day 35. My gracious and wise husband looked at me after the chapter was complete and said, "I agree that you are supposed to lay down your career in medical sales." I couldn't believe what I was hearing! I felt nervous and excited all at the same time.

I struggled with that decision for so long that I didn't waste time telling my bosses. In October 2015, I packed up my sweet company minivan and drove into the office to let my bosses know that I needed to resign, and I was freaking out. I cried out to God, *I don't want to do this! What if I'm making a mistake? God, will you please give me one more sign? Is this what you are calling me to do?*

It's important to note that he had given me hundreds of signs that I was supposed to quit my medical sales job. Yet, in his faithfulness, right after I cried out in desperation, a song came on my Christian music station. The words pierced my heart, but in the best way possible. It felt like God had amplified the lyrics, and it sounded almost like a megaphone coming through the speakers. The words reminded me that the leap of faith that I was about to take was obedience. I could trust him in the unknown, let go of my plans for myself, and trust in his plans. I could give up control.

A popular image floating around the Internet shows Jesus down on one knee by a little girl who is holding a teddy bear. In the picture, Jesus is holding out his hand, indicating to the little girl to give up her teddy bear. Clutching the teddy bear tightly and staring into Jesus's eyes, the little girl says to him, "But I love it, God." What the little girl doesn't see is that Jesus has a bigger and better teddy bear behind his back waiting to give her. With his arms stretched out, Jesus replies, "Trust me."

I was like the girl clutching the teddy bear. I was saying to Jesus, *But I want it, God! Let me keep my stressful, life-sucking job. Let me keep the money and perks. I don't want to give it up; it's my teddy bear, it's my comfort, it's all I know. I'm good at it. Please let me hang on to it.* But he was saying, *No, sweet child, trust me. I have something so much better.*

He sure did: a life filled with the proper priorities. My family came second to seeking God. Even though I needed to walk away from that career to learn a valuable lesson in priorities, he still gave me the desires of my heart. He knew I loved being an entrepreneur, and he catapulted my side business of photography to a whole new level.

In October 2017, while attending a women's conference in Texas, I felt another prompting: *Lay it down.* Instinctively, I knew that *lay it down* meant photography. Since I had been through this in my medical sales career, I knew right away that I needed to be obedient. But surrender is never easy. Giving up your teddy bear is always hard. This time God led me directly to Scripture. Genesis 22 tells the story of Abraham's faith being tested. I read the story in awe and wonder. God called Abraham to sacrifice his one and only son, whom he loved so much, as an offering to God. A heaven-sent angel intervened when he was about to kill his son with a knife. The angel told him to not lay a hand on the boy. Let's pause for a second to think about how intense it must have been for Abraham to hold a knife up to his son, only for an angel to show up and stop him right before he was about to follow through. I would have been sweating bullets. Talk about being saved by the bell. Could God have called it any closer? But what the angel said to Abraham after that is the best part of the story: "For now I know that you truly fear God. You have not withheld from me even your son, your only son" (Gen. 22:12 NLT). Then a ram showed up in the bushes, and Abraham sacrificed it instead of his son. The place where this all happened Abraham beautifully named Yahweh-Yireh, which means "the Lord will provide."

Abraham's faith inspired me. He loved God so much that he was willing to sacrifice his son. Talk about obedience and laying down control. If Abraham could walk in that type of obedience, then I could as well. After all, God wasn't asking me to sacrifice a child. However, I certainly loved the business. I had birthed the dream of the company from conception, being a solo entrepreneur, to later becoming a beautiful partnership with my dear friend where we had employees and hundreds of happy repeat clients. Our photography company was well-trusted, even among professional athletes and their families. I was very proud of what God had accomplished in the short time our photography company had been in business. To lay it down and completely walk away from it was a painful thing to do.

I also felt like God was testing my faith. Leaving the photography business to my partner meant that I would have no other income to help provide for our family. My husband had an excellent job and was the primary breadwinner, but my photography career was a nice cushion for the extras we liked to do in life. The act of leaving the company became my "Yahweh-Yireh" moment.

I'm happy to report that I was obedient. I am no longer pursuing photography, and the Lord never stopped providing for us. Currently, I am fully walking in my God-given purpose, which is writing, speaking, and leading in the arena of all things that have to do with fear and anxiety. I run a nonprofit called Fearless Unite—its mission is to set people free from fear and anxiety through God's Word. The pain that almost wiped me out is now my life's calling.

You may have a teddy bear you don't want to hand over to Jesus. What is it? Your job, a wayward child you are enabling, your finances, a relationship? I believe that every moment we don't surrender, we allow the enemy to steal precious moments from our life by worrying about things we cannot control. Worry is a byproduct of trying to control things. An old saying goes, "Worry is like a rocking chair; it's something to do, but it gets you nowhere." The Bible backs up that old saying: "So don't worry about tomorrow, for tomorrow will bring its own worries. Today's trouble is enough for today" (Matt. 6:34 NLT). I love how the *Life Application Bible Commentary* explains the verse: "Don't let worries about tomorrow affect your relationships with God today." Preparation and planning are wise. When we do that, it can alleviate worry because we have planned well. My takeaway from this scripture is there is always an opportunity to worry and always an opportunity to trust God. Which one will you choose?

Surrender is not weak—it is where strength lies. What do you say? It's time to wave that white flag—you're not waving it to give up. You're waving it to stand up for God.

- Commit to Jesus
- Commit to building your faith
- Commit your actions to the Lord
- Commit to laying down control

In these steps, you will find surrender. Let's not cheat either; let's have none of this partial surrender stuff. Let's fully commit all parts of our lives to the Lord. Peace is waiting for you on the other side of surrender.

# CHAPTER 12

# Comfort Others with the Comfort You Have Been Given

I remember the moment I felt called to share my anxiety journey like it was yesterday. It was warm and sunny on Mother's Day weekend in 2011—my family was outside enjoying a barbecue. I was dealing with anxiety considerably well and was in a great spot—body, soul, and spirit. Then suddenly, I felt a strong prompting while lounging on my chair on the driveway: *It's time to write about your experience with panic and anxiety.* Initially, I laughed it off. Who would want to hear all about my panic attacks? Nobody cares about that. Plus, I'm horrible at writing. I did very poorly in English, especially in spelling and grammar. I had the guts to ask my husband what he thought about the strong prompting. I should have known better than to share with my incredible and supportive husband. He immediately said, "You better get started."

## Me Too

I began to think about what it would look like to share my story. I consider myself a fast mover. If I feel called to do something, I don't waste time. Within a few hours, I had opened a free blogger account and began writing. There was so much to the story I decided to write it in parts. I posted Part 1 without checking grammar or having anyone look over the content. I chose my personal Facebook page to promote the blog. Laying myself bare, I didn't hold back. I was shocked by the responses. One by one, I was receiving feedback. Overwhelmingly, the reactions were, *me too.*

I needed to process; what did they mean, *me too*? Was I not the only one who struggled with panic attacks? How could this be, and why was no one talking about their struggles? Let's pause to read a scripture:

> He comforts us in all our troubles so that we can comfort others. When they are troubled, we will be able to give them the same comfort God has given us. For the more we suffer for Christ, the more God will shower us with his comfort through Christ. Even when we are weighed down with troubles, it is for your comfort and salvation! (2 Cor. 1:4–6 NLT)

Second Corinthians 1 directly confirms what I heard on that beautiful sunny day on the driveway. Sharing my story means I get to share the comfort God has given me. We should spread comfort like confetti. Talking openly about my pain and the comfort I have received from God is like pressing a pay-it-forward button. The person on the other side receives comfort for their pain, comfort that could ultimately lead to salvation.

Shortly after I posted Part 2 of my story, the pastor's wife at the church I attended contacted me and asked if I would do a video for a women's event and share my testimony. I couldn't believe that one simple act of obedience in writing the blog led to this much opportunity to comfort others. Not long after that, I spoke in front of five hundred women. I grew in opportunities to share until I heard very clearly, *It's time to start a support group.* Not understanding what that meant, I confided in a few friends for advice and support.

The first friend I talked to discouraged me. She spoke with her husband, who was someone I considered a spiritual giant in my life, and together their response was, "Aim longer before you fire. You are not ready to start a ministry." That advice crushed me. I took that advice to my husband. He took a moment to process it and confidently said, "No, if you aim too long, you will miss; it's time to start this ministry." Later, upon explaining the prompting to start a support group to another friend, she looked at me in disbelief. The Lord had told her the same thing, and she felt like it was supposed to be with me. We prayed about it, and, in no time at all, we held our first support group gathering at a local library in September 2015; thirty-six women came. We called the support group Fearless Women. The need was great, and the response was terrific; it confirmed our decision to obey. By December 2015, right before Christmas, Fearless Women attained nonprofit status.

The rapid growth of the meetings quickly made us outgrow the support group mindset. We became a pillar in our community for programing around fear and anxiety. In 2018, one of our meetings had over one thousand two hundred women in attendance. When you give your story to God, he gets the glory. Women were coming to find comfort from fear and anxiety, and they were leaving transformed by Jesus and were walking away saved.

I want to share three of my favorite Fearless Women testimonies with you. This salvation story is a tearjerker. A precious woman named Cassie was suffering from anxiety and fear. She noticed the videos I posted about Fearless Women because she was walking through her own hell with it. She was newly pregnant, single, and severely depressed and anxious. In her darkness, she considered if ending her life would be a viable solution to the pain she was enduring. She knew she could never go through with that, primarily because of the new life she had forming inside her. With a constant stream of negative thoughts, she wondered how she would care for a newborn. She thought about adoption. That didn't feel right either. In a desperate plea for comfort, she reached out to me. We met for coffee, and I had the amazing opportunity to lead her to Jesus.

The experience made her feel as though somebody had lifted an enormous burden from her shoulders. Peace began to flood her heart and mind. The fog of anxiety and depression started to dissipate in the months to come. She gave birth to a healthy and beautiful baby boy and asked me to be his godmother. As of 2022, Cassie is a key leader within our Fearless Women organization. She pioneered our merchandising department and now serves on our photography team. She is a loyal friend and cherished teammate.

The next story brings chills to my body every time I recall it. Despite being tortured by a past full of too many things to list, Natasha got tricked into attending a Fearless Women meeting. She walked in with a heavy heart due to her rebellious past. Her friend told her it was an anxiety meeting, but little did she know that Jesus had prepared an encounter with her. Everything the Fearless Women team said from the stage felt like a personal message to her broken heart during the entire night. After the closing song, a compelling force came over her, picked her up from her seat, and brought her to one of our prayer partners. Natasha dropped some profane language as she explained to our volunteer that she had no idea why she came up for prayer. With no judgment at all, our sweet prayer partner named Charity knew precisely why and led her through the salvation prayer. That moment in Natasha's life marked the start of healing and wholeness. Today, Natasha has given her whole life to Jesus. Through her broken past, she uses her gifts and talents to bring light to the kingdom of God.

Are you glowing brightly for Jesus like Natasha? I made a reel on Instagram not too long ago in which I portrayed two characters. The reel showed a woman feverishly attempting to hide her lamp under an office chair and another woman looking on, wondering why. The woman onlooker asked why she was trying to hide her light, to which the lamp-hiding lady said she didn't want anyone to see her light. The onlooker explained that she shouldn't hide her light and should instead let it shine.

Matthew 5:14–16 tells this same story. Let our good deeds shine so others can see and so we please our heavenly Father. When we follow Jesus, we should look different. Followers of Jesus should be such great ambassadors of him that people who are not following Jesus should be curious about our joy and peace.

I try to live a life that lets my light shine bright for Jesus as much as possible. Below is a good-deed story that led to an amazing Fearless Women moment. Remember, a biblical principle is that you reap what you sow. The story below tells how reaping goodness has a highly positive outcome.

## Fearlessness and the Power of God

Several years ago, my oldest son had kidney surgery. We had a nurse named Kim, who did a fantastic job dealing with my anxious thoughts and questions. She also cared well for Nolan, who had some severe pain during recovery; after all, he was the patient, not me. This hospital admission was an emotional time for our family because it was also the day we found out that Papa B's experimental treatment for his prostate cancer was not working. Kim felt like part of the family as she cared and loved for us the best way she knew how. After Nolan's discharge, I strongly felt that I was supposed to write to her supervisors and let them know how much we appreciated her care and exceptional work. I thought I would never see her again.

Fast-forward to a year later when Kim showed up at a Fearless meeting with her friend Jenny, who had also been tricked into coming. I'm not sure what is up with that, but it works, so I can't complain. We had an awkward exchange at first as Jenny introduced us. I don't forget faces, so I stared at her for a while and said, "I know you!" She agreed, and we went through the list of ways people figure out how they know each other. We figured it out when we got to the *Where do you work?* question. I hugged her and welcomed her to the Fearless Women event and told her I hoped she enjoyed it and that I was so glad to see her again. That evening, God performed a mighty work in her heart that snowballed into many extraordinary life changes.

Her soul needed a night of encouragement. Near the end, we asked anyone who needed prayer to stand. Much like Natasha, she felt a tug to stand. She told me later that her soul will never be the same after experiencing that moment. Her heart exploded with the fullness of God's grace and forgiveness, and for the first time, she truly felt worthy of his love.

Here is the rest of Kim's testimony:

At the very end of the evening, they announced the date of their first retreat. I knew I *had* to go. When we got in the car, I remembered that Christy had written me up for a "Daisy Award," an opportunity for families to recognize nurses who have provided excellent care. I found my Daisy Award that night, and it was the last sign I needed to know this was more than me that brought me to Fearless.

A few months later, Jenny and I walked into the doors of a Branson, Missouri, retreat house, knowing only a few other people. March 3 through 5, 2022, my life was officially changed. The talks spoke everything to my hurting, grieving, broken heart and soul. I found a love for Christ again. I found my people, my faith family—a bunch of beautiful, godly women who have very human struggles. Fearless has changed my life in so many ways that there aren't even words. I am healing, searching, learning, and loving in ways I never imagined, and I wouldn't be in this place without Fearless and the power of God.

None of this would have been possible if I had not been obedient to the call to share my story. Please don't mistake these words for pride; none of these stories would have happened without God's amazing grace. Yet, God partners with us to share our stories for his glory to the world. That's why your obedience to share your story matters—your pain has a purpose. Our calling is to comfort others with the same comfort God has given us. Pay it forward; it's that simple.

## The Benefits of Helping Others

What you focus on grows. If all you do is sit around and think about your fears, you will become anxious and depressed. Working hard with the tools I have given you can prevent fear and anxiety from consuming you. Another step you can take to avoid anxiety flareups is to help others deal with fear. Most people think they must be worry-free and exempt from panic attacks before they can help someone dealing with anxiety. That could not be further from the truth. Your struggle with anxiety is what qualifies you to help. There is nothing worse than asking for help with anxiety from someone who doesn't understand it. You are more equipped to help others if you struggle with anxiety because you will likely have a greater sense of empathy.

Interestingly, helping others can improve mental health, lower stress, increase happiness, and boost confidence. Scripture also backs helping others. We have addressed 2 Corinthians 1:4–6, but are there any other scriptures to support helping others? There sure are!

- "Carry each other's burdens, and in this way you will fulfill the law of Christ." (Gal. 6:2 NIV)
- "My command is this: Love each other as I have loved you." (John 15:12 NIV)
- "In the same way, let your light shine before others, that they may see your good deeds and glorify your Father in heaven." (Matt. 5:16 NIV)
- "Do not withhold good from those to whom it is due, when it is in your power to act." (Prov. 3:27 NIV)
- "In everything I have shown you that, by working hard, we must help the weak. In this way we remember the Lord Jesus' words: 'It is more blessed to give than to receive.'" (Acts 20:35 CEB)

Having the opportunity to help others benefits us. Have you heard that it's better to give than to receive? The above scriptures have a strong theme of that idea. Let me encourage you to think about these scriptures and the categories of people God has brought into your life. Are there people who battle with fear and anxiety? I bet that without much work, you would be able to identify some. What if God is calling you to help them? It could be the woman you carpool with regularly, your manager at work, a friend in Bible study, your sister-in-law, or the acquaintance you wave to in the school pickup line who needs to see Jesus more clearly.

What if you are the person God will use to help them over-come anxiety and walk in a more surrendered life? If you are bold and brave with how anxiety has impacted your life, it might cause a ripple effect of healing in their life. Sharing is caring, and it feels great to do it!

Tell people what God has done to meet you in your pain; remember, your pain has a purpose. Just share your story with authenticity. Our tests in life can become our strongest testimo-nies, and when we steward our testimony well, it changes lives. Changed lives make disciples. Being a disciple doesn't mean we are perfect—such a life doesn't exist; being a disciple simply means we commit to following Jesus and practicing his ways. It's how the news about Jesus gets presented to unbelievers through God's people. All who call Jesus Lord need to take this calling seriously. We are not all pastors, worship leaders, or evangelists, but all of us have gifts that help us fulfill the Great Commission.

## Personality Profiles and Spiritual Gifts

Chances are you have taken a personality test before. There are many good ones out there. One of my favorites is the Enneagram. That test and its resources have helped me become a better wife, mother, friend, leader, and, most importantly, a less anxious individual. You might wonder how a personality test helped me become less anxious. I have much clarity on this topic that I'm excited to share. The two things that bring me the most anxiety in life are relationship conflicts and health issues. After identifying that relationship anxiety was a weakness of mine, I set out to find extra help and wisdom on how to deal with people well.

Several years ago, I found myself in a horrible argument with an assistant on the Fearless team, and I left feeling misunderstood and highly undervalued. I'm positive she did, too. For the life of me, I couldn't figure out what was going on. How did things get so bad so quickly? I prayed, read my Bible, journaled, and felt called to reach out to a mentor, someone from my "pouring" category. She asked me if I had ever heard of the Enneagram. At that point, I hadn't and even had a hard time pronouncing it. I began to study the way God created me through some of the tools and resources God's people have developed, like Beth McCord's Enneagram courses and books. Beth uses a Christ-centered approach in her teachings. Through her work, I discovered why I had a fear of betrayal. Beth's resources pegged me so accurately on how I respond when I'm healthy and unhealthy that it blew my mind. I finally had language for how I had felt for so long but couldn't explain. The long-term goal is that we become the best versions of ourselves with the help of Jesus, which is the sanctification process. Through prayer and counseling, I could find freedom from the fear of betrayal and become healthier mentally and spiritually. When triggered during a conflict, I know what to look for now, and it doesn't turn into full-blown anxiety.

I found even greater freedom when I examined how God made other people. Understanding how their strengths and weaknesses interact with mine was fascinating and incredibly helpful. The book that led me to such insights was *The Path Between Us* by Suzanne Stabile. Everyone sees the world through different-colored glasses. Understanding, respecting, and having patience with God's people and their unique personalities helps you be a stronger and more peaceful person.

I'm grateful the Lord led me to Christ-centered tools written by Beth and Suzanne. However, like any tool, there is room for error. I have seen people take these tests and consider them the end-all and be-all. You must remember that tests can be wrong, and the people who offer these tools are not God. Taking a personality test can be just as inaccurate as taking a pregnancy test, so you need to keep that in mind. Also, don't just take the results at face value.

Analyze your findings, and submit them to God in prayer. God's Word contains the most incredible wisdom we can ever find. The Holy Spirit is the best mentor, leader, and teacher—nothing else compares. Sometimes, the Holy Spirit will lead you to tools and resources to further your spiritual growth process. There is nothing wrong with that. Tools in the hands of God are powerful. After taking a personality test, the most important thing to remember is that your identity is not a personality profile type. Your identity is a child of God, created in the image of God for good works, which he prepared for you before the beginning of time.

Since God prepared good works for you before time began, it is helpful to understand your gifts. The Bible has a lot to say about spiritual gifts. One area of the Bible that breaks this down is 1 Corinthians 12. I highly recommend that you stop now and read that chapter. Then take a quick quiz to find out what your spiritual gifts are. Lifeway.com has brilliant testing tools and resources. Just pull up its website and search "spiritual gifts." Here is a list of different gifts to whet your appetite:

- Leadership (Rom. 12:8)
- Administration (1 Cor. 12:28)
- Teaching (1 Cor. 12:28; Rom. 12:7; Eph. 4:11)
- Words of Knowledge (1 Cor. 12:28)
- Wisdom (1 Cor. 12:28)
- Prophecy (1 Cor. 12:10; Rom. 12:6)
- Discernment (1 Cor. 12:10)
- Exhortation (Rom. 12:8)
- Shepherding (Eph. 4:11)
- Faith (1 Cor. 12:9)
- Evangelism (Eph. 4:11)
- Apostleship (1 Cor. 12:28; Eph. 4:11)
- Service/Helping (1 Cor. 12:28; Rom. 12:7)

- Mercy (Rom. 12:8)
- Giving (Rom. 12:8)
- Hospitality (1 Pet. 4:9)

My top five gifts are teaching, leadership, administration, words of knowledge, and discernment. I used to feel bad that I didn't feel called to help in the kitchen. Preparing food for parties gave me anxiety. Trying to bake, cook, and be hospitable was like shoving a square peg into a round hole. It just didn't fit. When I discovered my gifts, I felt free knowing hospitality was not my gift. Suddenly, it all made sense. I gave up trying to be Betty Crocker, and I let my friends with that gift rise to the occasion. When I attempt to be someone I am not, I always feel anxious.

Turning my pain into purpose has been one of my greatest joys. I would have never dreamed that experiencing a nervous breakdown would turn into leading a nonprofit called Fearless Women (we now operate under the name Fearless Unite). I certainly would have never guessed it would turn into a book either. Yet here you and I are. I'm teaching through the pain, and hopefully, you're feeling comforted.

God has a plan for your pain, too—use it for God's glory; it's so worth it. Then, don't be ashamed of your past, and don't be ashamed of how God made you. Explore your gifts, and look forward to growing. Take time to study how God has made you; it's valuable to discover. Since you need community in life, also take time to learn how God has made others. Understanding yourself, others, and spiritual gifts will help you discover your purpose and live a more peaceful and fulfilling life.

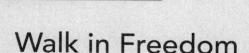

# CHAPTER 13

# Walk in Freedom

I clearly remember the day when I blocked a panic attack for the first time instead of dodging it. It felt remarkable to stop the fear before it stopped me. I was walking through a major conflict with someone and was also sick. The two biggest things that trigger me were happening at the same time. I didn't dodge the fear bullets, I stopped them, and I was so excited! I was able to stop the snowball of thoughts and redirect them to God's promises. I took a walk, which calmed the adrenaline that was rushing in. Then, I prayed while I walked, and peace came over me. Just like that, the panic passed without harm.

What did I do? I stopped trying to control the situation and let God be God. Psalm 46:10 famously says, "Be still, and know that I am God" (NIV). This scripture calls us to stop striving and let God fight on our behalf, to rest in him and surrender. Being still is not a passive approach; it's the best approach possible. Too often, we strive to solve a problem with our strength when God already has the answers. Being still and knowing means to admit you are not God and to submit to and trust in the God of the universe, who is all-knowing, powerful, and ever-present in times of trouble. Realizing that I need to fully trust God has been one of the most important factors in overcoming my fear and anxiety.

Learning to stop panic and anxiety has taken years of practice and discipline, but now I know it is possible. I'm living proof of it. I'm happy to report my panic attacks are few and far between. The label of severe panic and anxiety disorder is now in the past. I don't require medication anymore for anxiety and depression. I realize that my being off my medication while you may still require medication might stir up some mixed emotions. Please feel no shame for needing help. Stay on it for as long as God calls you to. If you are hoping to get off medication, pray without ceasing. The decision to come off medication for mental health diagnoses is an outcome that you should weigh thoroughly with your clinical team. You should never stop anxiety or depression medication cold turkey. There is a process of weaning that is critical if you want to be successful in coming off your medication.

## Not Another Self-Help Book

It took me a long time to realize that I didn't need to feed and follow fear and anxiety for one second longer. You may have some hard but hopeful work ahead of you to do that, but I believe you can overcome as well.

I hope that my struggle and my story have inspired and encouraged you, but hope is not a strategy. What we need is something more concrete. The Bible explains, "Now faith is the substance of things hoped for, the evidence of things not seen" (Heb 11:1 NKJV). Faith without action is dead. Hoping for a better tomorrow doesn't do anything, but putting faith in motion does. The surest way to defeat fear and build your faith is to follow Jesus closely. A better life has nothing to do with achievements, success, or material things, but it does have everything to do with surrender and obedience to Jesus Christ. No pill, essential oil, person, book, or program will lead you to freedom. Only Jesus can. The other suggestions are just tools surrendered in the hands of our mighty God.

I don't want our journey together to be just another "self-help" book you have lying on the nightstand that motivated you but created no lasting change. As we discussed, self-help is no help at all. Your help comes from the Lord, not from self. My deepest desire is that God is meeting you through the pages of this book and that you are experiencing many breakthrough moments that grant you freedom from fear and anxiety. I would be honored if you would share those with me. Send me your freedom from fear and anxiety stories to christy@fearlessunite.com.

## Final Send-Off

You get what you put in, or, in other words, you reap what you sow. Fear is not the story you want to reap. Instead, you want to sow a life filled with faith and trust in Jesus. This brings to mind my favorite practical and applicable scripture on worry. Every time I read this scripture, I learn something new about fortifying my faith and overcoming fear. I pray that these words from Jesus will do the same for you:

> I tell you not to worry about everyday life—whether
> you have enough food and drink, or enough clothes to
> wear. Isn't life more than food, and your body more than
> clothing? Look at the birds. They don't plant or harvest
> or store food in barns, for your heavenly Father feeds
> them. And aren't you far more valuable to him than they
> are? Can all your worries add a single moment to your

life? And why worry about your clothing? Look at the lilies of the field and how they grow. They don't work or make their clothing, yet Solomon in all his glory was not dressed as beautifully as they are. And if God cares so wonderfully for wildflowers that are here today and thrown into the fire tomorrow, he will certainly care for you. Why do you have so little faith? So don't worry about these things, saying, "What will we eat? What will we drink? What will we wear?" These things dominate the thoughts of unbelievers, but your heavenly Father already knows all your needs. Seek the Kingdom of God above all else, and live righteously, and he will give you everything you need. So don't worry about tomorrow, for tomorrow will bring its own worries. Today's trouble is enough for today. (Matt. 6:25–35 NLT)

Friend, don't be deceived by the worries of this life and the wealth of this world. Those things dominate the thoughts of unbelievers. The wealth of this life is fading, and you can't take it with you. This world is not our home. Heaven is. The promise of an eternal glorious life in heaven has weakened the sting of death. If death is no longer something to fear, what do we have to fear? What's the point of worrying? God already knows what we need, and he cares. Decide now that God's plan for your life is the most important thing you will ever accomplish. Commit yourself to the kingdom of God, and live a life of biblical success, not worldly success.

I know life is not always picture perfect or crystal clear, so I want to leave you with some "ready" statements. I put together twenty-five of them. These statements will summarize what you have learned in this book so you can confidently walk in freedom from fear and anxiety. It will be helpful to write these out, memorize them, and keep them visible every day. Then, speak these truths out loud and often. The devil can't read your thoughts, but he can hear your words. What are you going to declare today? Faith statements or fear statements? Peace depends on how you perceive fear. Will you speak fearful words or faithful words over yourself?

- I will not trust in my own insight; instead, I will walk in God's wisdom. (Adapted from Proverbs 28:26)
- I will not be conformed to the patterns of this world but be transformed by the renewing of my mind. (Adapted from Romans 12:2)
- I lift my eyes up; my help comes from God. (Adapted from Psalm 121:1–2)
- I do not operate out of the spirit of fear because God has given me a sound mind. (Adapted from 2 Timothy 1:7)
- I will not be afraid, for God is close beside me. His rod and staff protect and comfort me. (Adapted from Psalm 23:4)
- I will not walk in fear; I will walk in God's love. (Adapted from 1 John 4:18)
- I will not fail; God is within me. (Adapted from Psalm 46:5)
- I declare this about the Lord: he alone is my refuge, my place of safety; he is my God, and I trust him. (Adapted from Psalm 91:2)
- I will take time to rest and be with God alone. (Adapted from Mark 6:30–32)
- I will live at peace with everyone as far as it depends on me. (Adapted from Romans 12:18)
- I am valuable. (Adapted from Luke 12:7)
- I am forgiven. (Adapted from Psalm 103:10–12)
- I will love you, Lord, with all my heart, soul, and mind. (Adapted from Matthew 22:37)
- I will not listen to the enemy's lies. (Adapted from John 8:44)

- I will demolish arguments and every idea that sets itself up against the knowledge of God and capture every thought to make it line up with the power of God's Word. (Adapted from 2 Corinthians 10:5)
- I will not seek the approval of man. (Adapted from Galatians 1:10)
- I will not be corrupted by bad company; I will surround myself with godly people. (Adapted from 1 Corinthians 15:33)
- I will draw near to God, and he will draw near to me. (Adapted from James 4:8)
- I will be still and trust God. (Adapted from Psalm 46:10)
- I will be strong in the Lord, putting on the whole armor of God every day. (Adapted from Ephesians 6)
- I will work out my salvation with respect and honor to God. (Adapted from Philippians 2:12–13)
- I will not worry about anything, but instead, I will pray about everything. (Adapted from Philippians 4:6)
- I will have peace in God. (Adapted from John 16:33)
- I will go and make disciples. (Adapted from Matthew 28:19)
- I will shine my light bright for Jesus. (Adapted from Matthew 5:14–16)

With these ready statements, the knowledge you have gained in this book, and the Holy Spirit's power working through your precious salvation, you are equipped to fight. God has a clear destiny for you, and it's not a life disrupted by continual fear and annoying anxiety. I declare that the fullness of God's love is activated in your life—the pressure is lifted. You are no longer a slave to fear. You are a child of the holy King, and God has called you to be unafraid. The cross makes you fearless. Now walk in that freedom.

# STUDY GUIDE

## Breakthrough Run Through

- The applause of men became the approval my soul lived for.

- Success and achievement were not just an option for me; they were my drugs of choice.

- Though successful in many worldly ways, my walk with God was far from successful.

- It felt weak to rely on anyone other than myself.

- Your insight lacks clarity and purpose when it's not submitted to an all-knowing God.

- Google is a dangerous tool in the hands of an anxious person. Google is not God.

- The world measures success by attaining wealth, favor, influence, and power. The Bible says success occurs by obeying God.

- We shortchange ourselves when we rely only on ourselves.

- "We were designed for camel travel, not supersonic jet behavior." —Archibald Hart

- A problem arises when our strengths become God replacements instead of God "reliances," making our strength into the idol we worship instead of God.

- The world's way creates stressed-out, anxious, depressed, but "successful" people. Renewing our minds to a higher way of thinking promises peace and slows our frantic pace, redefining a "successful" life.

### SCRIPTURES

- "Those who trust their own insight are foolish, but anyone who walks in wisdom is safe" (Prov. 28:26 NLT).

- "Plans go wrong for lack of advice; many advisers bring success" (Prov. 15:22 NLT).

- "Observe the requirements of the LORD your God, and follow all his ways. Keep the decrees, commands, regulations, and laws written in the Law of Moses so that you will be successful in all you do and wherever you go" (1 Kings 2:3 NLT).

- "Do not be conformed to this age, but be transformed by the renewing of your mind, so that you may discern what is the good, pleasing, and perfect will of God" (Rom. 12:2 CSB).

# Reflection Questions

1. In what ways do you chase after the approval of others?

2. What are the unhealthy ways in which success and achievement invade your life?

3. How would you rate your walk with God?

4. Do you feel like you are the hero of your own story? Explain.

5. Do you feel like Google is a dangerous tool in the hands of an anxious person? Why or why not?

6. The online edition of the *Merriam-Webster Dictionary* defines success as "the attainment of wealth, favor, or eminence." The Bible's view of success states, "Observe the requirements of the LORD your God, and follow all his ways. Keep the decrees, commands, regulations, and laws written in the Law of Moses so that you will be successful in all you do and wherever you go" (1 Kings 2:3 NLT). How do you view success?

7. How do we shortchange ourselves when we rely only on ourselves?

8. Forty-six percent of Americans will meet the criteria for a diagnosable mental health condition sometime in their life, and half of those people develop conditions by age fourteen. Christy linked this problem to running our lives at supersonic jet speed. Do you agree or disagree?

9. Do you have room to improve and redefine success in your life? Why or why not?

10. How can renewing our minds bring peace?

## Chapter 2: The Label I Never Asked For

### Breakthrough Run Through

- Education can help you be a better human being.

- Medical professionals say panic attacks don't last long. That's true, but each one leaves a forever imprint on your soul.

- Panic and anxiety will make you vulnerable, whether you like it or not.

- Panic and anxiety mess with your entire body. It's just as much physical as mental.

- Our world teaches us to rely on ourselves to fix our problems and depend on ourselves to meet our needs. That's self-help. But the truth is, self-help is no help at all.

- When you're down, there aren't many places to look except up.

- Self-reliance failed me, so I tried surrender of self. I surrendered to a God who loves me and desires to free me of my fears and anxiety.

- All the success I gained and achievements I earned became powerless in the face of severe panic and anxiety.

- When trials come without your permission, they change you.

- I knew heaven was higher than the earth, but I didn't live like it.

- So much fear and anxiety come from our worldly, human views.

- Since his ways *are* higher, we must look at our situations and circumstances from God's higher viewpoint rather than from our limited human one.

### SCRIPTURES

- "I lift up my eyes to the mountains—where does my help come from? My help comes from the LORD, the Maker of heaven and earth" (Ps. 121:1–2 NIV).

- "'For My thoughts are not your thoughts, Nor are your ways My ways,' says the LORD. 'For as the heavens are higher than the earth, So are My ways higher than your ways, and My thoughts than your thoughts'" (Isa. 55:8–9 NKJV).

- "Get away from me, Satan! You are a dangerous trap to me. You are seeing things merely from a human point of view, not from God's" (Matt. 16:23 NLT).

- "God is our refuge and strength, a very present help in trouble" (Ps. 46:1 KJV).

## Reflection Questions

1. Are you educated on anxiety? How can you take steps today to learn more about it?

2. How does relying on self-help only complicate a diagnosis of anxiety?

3. Where does your help come from if it doesn't come from you?

4. How do trials change your priorities?

5. How often are you guilty of living life with an earthly viewpoint instead of a heavenly one? Explain.

6. How do we shift our focus higher, to God's way?

7. Are you currently believing the lie that the world would be better off without you? If so, what steps can you take to get help today?

## Chapter 3: Not Me—I'm Always in Control

### Breakthrough Run Through

- Nothing stops you faster than a diagnosis that slows you down.

- A truth that contradicts itself can no longer be true.

- I can't live a truth separate from someone else and we both be right.

- Lies often sound good and are believable but are packed with poison.

- There is a big difference between healthy planning versus the disorder of manifesting control in your life.

- Control is exhausting, and it comes with a high price.

- The world offers no accolades to surrender; in fact, it frowns on it.

- Surrender is a strength.

- It was time to make him my first response, not my last resort.

- Fans will often turn into followers when they realize their fandom doesn't buy anything but fear.

- Salvation is a decision. Surrender is a commitment.

- You can know the story of Jesus but not believe in it.

## SCRIPTURES

- "I am the way and the truth and the life. No one comes to the Father except through me" (John 14:6 NIV).

- "Those who trust in themselves are fools, but those who walk in wisdom are kept safe" (Prov. 28:26 NIV).

- "In their hearts humans plan their course, but the LORD establishes their steps" (Prov. 16:9 NIV).

- "My sheep listen to my voice; I know them, and they follow me" (John 10:27 NLT).

- "If you declare with your mouth, 'Jesus is Lord,' and believe in your heart that God raised him from the dead, you will be saved" (Rom. 10:9 NIV).

- "For God so loved the world that he gave his one and only Son, that whoever believes in him shall not perish but have eternal life" (John 3:16 NIV).

## Reflection Questions

1. Describe some ways anxiety slows your life down.

2. Do you believe you are the hero of your own story? Explain.

3. Do you believe in absolute truth? Why or why not?

4. How can believing lies become dangerous in your life?

5. Do you hold plans loosely? Are you willing to lay plans down if the Lord leads you in a new direction?

6. List your controlling ways. Is the outcome of those statements you just identified bringing peace?

7. What is peace?

8. Are you a fan or follower of Jesus? Explain.

## Chapter 4: Fear the Bigger Pandemic

### Breakthrough Run Through

- Separating our physical, spiritual, and mental health is *not* working.

- Keeping church for Sunday mornings, doctors for offices and hospitals, and psychologists and psychiatrists for comfy couches is only doing a major disservice to our lives.

- Body, soul, and spirit need equal parts of "air" to function correctly.

- We walk in the peace of God by knowing the Word of God.

- The goal isn't to cultivate a life free of fear; such a life doesn't exist. It's to learn how to fear less.

- Our bodies need balance; too much or too little of something will create problems.

- You can believe in miracles while taking practical steps toward healing.

- Sometimes God will lead us through a problem to a promise he wants to teach us.

- God allows medications to be a part of our stories here on earth.

- Taking medication does not mean you lack faith.

- Sometimes you must go back to plow forward. An arrow on a bow needs to be pulled back to find the speed and strength to fly. So does the arrow of your life.

- As I got to know God's truth in my life, it transformed me from the inside out.

- Medicine is not a Band-Aid; it's a tool.

- My hope and foundation are in Jesus, not Celexa.

- Have grace with your healing process. Don't rush it, and don't delay it either.

- Jesus, seeing a doctor, and Christian therapy are the top three things; in that order, I overcame severe panic and anxiety disorder.

## SCRIPTURES

- "For God hath not given us the spirit of fear; but of power, and of love, and of a sound mind" (2 Tim. 1:7 KJV).

- "There is no fear in love. But perfect love drives out fear, because fear has to do with punishment. The one who fears is not made perfect in love" (1 John 4:18 NIV).

- "So do not fear, for I am with you; do not be dismayed, for I am your God. I will strengthen you and help you; I will uphold you with my righteous right hand" (Isa. 41:10 NIV).

- "Even when I walk through the darkest valley, I will not be afraid, for you are close beside me. Your rod and your staff protect and comfort me" (Ps. 23:4 NLT).

- "So be strong and courageous! Do not be afraid and do not panic before them. For the Lord your God will personally go ahead of you. He will neither fail you nor abandon you" (Deut. 31:6 NLT).

- "Suddenly, a fierce storm struck the lake, with waves breaking into the boat. But Jesus was sleeping. The disciples went and woke him up, shouting, 'Lord, save us! We're going to drown!' Jesus responded, 'Why are you afraid? You have so little faith!' Then he got up and rebuked the wind and waves, and suddenly there was a great calm" (Matt. 8:24–26 NLT).

- "God is within her, she will not fall; God will help her at break of day" (Ps. 46:5 NIV).

- "They will have no fear of bad news; their hearts are steadfast, trusting in the Lord" (Ps. 112:7 NIV).

- "God is our refuge and strength, an ever-present help in trouble. Therefore we will not fear, though the earth give way and the mountains fall into the heart of the sea, though its waters roar and foam and the mountains quake with their surging" (Ps. 46:1–3 NIV).

- "Those who live in the shelter of the Most High will find rest in the shadow of the Almighty. This I declare about the LORD: He alone is my refuge, my place of safety; he is my God, and I trust him. For he will rescue you from every trap and protect you from deadly disease. He will cover you with his feathers. He will shelter you with his wings. His faithful promises are your armor and protection. Do not be afraid of the terrors of the night, nor the arrow that flies in the day. Do not dread the disease that stalks in darkness, nor the disaster that strikes at midday. Though a thousand fall at your side, though ten thousand are dying around you, these evils will not touch you" (Ps. 91:1–7 NLT).

- "Every good and perfect gift is from above" (James 1:17 NIV).

## Reflection Questions

1. How could a balanced approach to all three parts of your being help overcome anxiety?

2. What are the ways you care for your physical health over spiritual and mental health?

3. What steps can you take to balance your physical, spiritual, and mental health?

4. How can negative thoughts hurt your body? How do positive thoughts contribute to a healthier you?

5. What is the healthy balance between faith and medication?

6. Why would putting medication on a pedestal create more fear and anxiety in your life?

7. How can you believe in miracles while taking practical steps toward healing?

8. Is there a past area of your life you need to work on to plow forward into health?

9. How is knowing God's Word transformative?

10. What do you run to before you run to Jesus?

## Chapter 5: Smoke Alarms

### Breakthrough Run Through

- Smoke alarms come with built-in benefits to which we should begin paying attention.

- Everyone's body reacts differently when panic and anxiety are present. Resist the urge to compare anxiety stories.

- We all have different thresholds for stress.

- God is faithful to provide when you trust him.

- Lack of sleep is a breeding ground for anxiety.

- Being so busy that you can't get the recommended seven to nine hours of sleep isn't a cool thing; it's a stupid thing.

- I turn to Jesus's examples when I start to believe the lie that self-care is not holy.

- Far too often, we rush into things and wind up depleting ourselves of energy that God never asked us to spend.

- Time alone with God cannot be taken away by the pressures of this world.

- "But Jesus often withdrew to the wilderness for prayer" (Luke 5:16 NLT).

- Jesus isn't a stuffy high priest who commands us to do things without experiencing them himself.

- Sorrow takes a lot out of you. We cannot just hide from our pain. We must process it with God.

- Our works are not greater than our relationship with Jesus.

- Spending time in solitude with God to refresh your soul is not selfish; it is necessary to survive.

- Many of us stay in burning buildings for far too long.

- "You must choose wisely who you pull closely."
  —Kristin Bonin

- Any loss of peace you may be experiencing must be evaluated and brought to Jesus.

- Refusing to hit conflict head-on and quickly will keep smoke alarms going off regularly.

- Ignorance is not bliss.

- Smoke alarm steps:

  - Assess the situation.

  - Care for yourself and *then* your loved ones.

  - Call for help.

  - Remove yourself from the situation.

## SCRIPTURES

- Matthew 4 and Luke 4 (Jesus takes forty days and nights in the wilderness.)

- "But Jesus often withdrew to the wilderness for prayer" (Luke 5:16 NLT).

- "One day soon afterward Jesus went up on a mountain to pray, and he prayed to God all night. At daybreak he called together all of his disciples and chose twelve of them to be apostles" (Luke 6:12–13 NLT).

- "He left in a boat to a remote area to be alone" (Matt. 14:13 NLT).

- "He walked away, about a stone's throw, and knelt down and prayed, 'Father, if you are willing, please take this cup of suffering away from me. Yet I want your will to be done, not mine'" (Luke 22:41–42 NLT).

- "The apostles returned to Jesus from their ministry tour and told him all they had done and taught. Then Jesus said, 'Let's go off by ourselves to a quiet place and rest awhile.' He said this because there were so many people coming and going that Jesus and his apostles didn't even have time to eat. So they left by boat for a quiet place, where they could be alone" (Mark 6:30–32 NLT).

- "Therefore, since we are surrounded by such a huge crowd of witnesses to the life of faith, let us strip off every weight that slows us down, especially the sin that so easily trips us up. And let us run with endurance the race God has set before us" (Heb. 12:1 NLT).

- "If your brother or sister sins, go and point out their fault, just between the two of you. If they listen to you, you have won them over. But if they will not listen, take one or two others along, so that 'every matter may be established by the testimony of two or three witnesses.' If they still refuse to listen, tell it to the church; and if they refuse to listen even to the church, treat them as you would a pagan or a tax collector" (Matt. 18:15–17 NIV).

- "If it is possible, as far as it depends on you, live at peace with everyone" (Rom. 12:18 NIV).

## Reflection Questions

1. What smoke alarms do you face regularly?

2. Do you see how comparing your stress threshold to someone else's could be unhealthy? Why?

3. Take an inventory of your current commitments. Is it possible that you are too busy helping people? Did Jesus ask you to do all the helping you are doing?

4. What if we were more intentional at hiding from people to get wisdom, rest, and peace our soul needs so we can handle the people God has entrusted to us? In what ways could you start taking better care of your soul to get alone with God?

5. Are you hiding pain from God? Explain.

6. Do you run toward conflict? What conflicts are you facing that you need to address?

7. Which smoke alarm step do you do best?

   a. Assess the situation.

   b. Care for yourself and *then* your loved ones.

   c. Call for help.

   d. Remove yourself from the situation.

## Chapter 6: Perfect Love Casts Out Fear

### Breakthrough Run Through

- Until I truly learned to rest in God's love, I continued to significantly struggle with fear and anxiety.

- You need to deeply know his love to cast out fear.

- His love is deep, but his forgiveness for your sins is deeper.

- Sometimes the simple yet profound answer to your questions and trials in life is: God's ways are higher.

- Jesus understands your most profound, darkest moments and everyday mess-ups.

- Fear is counterfeit love.

- Where fear is operating, love cannot freely flow.

- Concern moves you to action, and worry stops the action.

- We should all have a healthy fear for our deep and great God.

- Americans are stressed out and anxious because most of us are unresponsive to the most important tool that can bring us peace.

- Vulnerability with God is a vehicle that he uses to heal us.

### SCRIPTURES

- "He does not punish us for all our sins; he does not deal harshly with us, as we deserve. For his unfailing love toward those who fear him is as great as the height of the heavens above the earth. He has removed our sins as far from us as the east is from the west" (Ps. 103:10–12 NLT).

- "'For my thoughts are not your thoughts, neither are your ways my ways,' declares the LORD. 'As the heavens are higher than the earth, so are my ways higher than your ways and my thoughts than your thoughts'" (Isa. 55:8–9 NIV).

- "Indeed, the very hairs of your head are all numbered. Do not fear; you are worth more than many sparrows" (Luke 12:7 NIV).

- "So then, since we have a great High Priest who has entered heaven, Jesus the Son of God, let us hold firmly to what we believe. This High Priest of ours understands our weaknesses, for he faced all of the same testings we do, yet he did not sin" (Heb. 4:14–15 NLT).

- "And may you have the power to understand, as all God's people should, how wide, how long, how high, and how deep his love is" for you (Eph. 3:18 NLT).

- "There is no fear in love. But perfect love drives out fear, because fear has to do with punishment. The one who fears is not made perfect in love" (1 John 4:18 NIV).

- "The Fear of the LORD is the fountain of life, turning a person from the snares of death" (Prov. 14:27 NIV).

- "For the word of God is alive and active. Sharper than any double-edged sword, it penetrates even to dividing soul and spirit, joints and marrow; it judges the thoughts and attitudes of the heart" (Heb. 4:12 NIV).

- "*I'm hurting*, Lord—will you forget me forever? How much longer, Lord? Will you look the other way when I'm in need?

How much longer must I cling to this constant grief? I've endured this shaking of my soul. So how much longer will my enemy have the upper hand? Take a good look at me, Yahweh, my God, and answer me! Breathe your life into my spirit. Bring light to my eyes in this pitch-black darkness or I will sleep the sleep of death. Don't let my enemy proclaim, 'I've prevailed over him.' For all my adversaries will celebrate when I fall. I have always trusted in your kindness, *so answer me.* I will spin in a circle of joy when your salvation lifts me up. I will sing my song of joy to you, Yahweh, for in all of this you have strengthened my soul. My enemies say that I have no Savior, but I know that I have one in you!" (Ps. 13:1–6 TPT).

## Reflection Questions

1. How does understanding the love of God help you overcome fear?

2. Do you question God's love for you? Explain.

3. Do you pay attention to the value God brings to your life? Explain.

4. What scriptures from this chapter help you understand God's love?

5. What are the types of fear Christy described? Do you fear God with awe and reverence?

6. Do you know the difference between God's voice and Satan's voice? Explain.

7. Do you tell God your fears?

## Chapter 7: Catch the Snowball

## Breakthrough Run Through

- Our thoughts have a lot to do with the anxiety that manifests.

- Do you realize that there has been a strategic plan to destroy our trust and connection with God since the beginning of time?

- Your thoughts can sink you or make you soar.

- Don't you want to rise above any crafty thoughts Satan sets up against the power of God?

- Fasting drops us to our knees in prayer and allows us to connect with Jesus in a way our soul so desperately needs.

- Satan can't read your mind, but he is aware of your actions.

- We would be prepared for more battles if fasting and prayer were priorities in our lives.

- Satan knows Scripture. The question is, does he know it better than you do?

- Your thoughts matter.

- When I rewire toxic thoughts diligently, I fall prey to anxiety attacks far less.

- We can recognize our negative feelings and still choose to make positive choices with our emotions.

- You can't overcome something you don't first acknowledge.

- The light of God's love can't shine on the dark thoughts you think if they remain hidden in your mind.

- We need to recognize the themes of negative thoughts before they snowball out of control.

- We can't just recognize negative thoughts. We must take it a step further and replace them.

- We can speak negatively or positively. Recite God's Word, not Satan's lies.

- Repetition makes renewing your mind easier over time.

- You must be ruthless and refuse to give up.

## SCRIPTURES

- "Love the Lord your God with all your heart and with all your soul and with all your mind" (Matt. 22:37 NIV).

- "The thief comes only to steal and kill and destroy; I have come that they may have life, and have it to the full" (John 10:10 NIV).

- "You must not eat from the tree of the knowledge of good and evil, for when you eat from it you will certainly die" (Gen. 2:17 NIV).

- "Did God really say, 'You must not eat from any tree in the garden'?" (Gen. 3:1 NIV).

- "Then Jesus was led by the Spirit into the wilderness to be tempted by the devil. After fasting forty days and forty nights, he was hungry. The tempter came to him and said, 'If you are the Son of God, tell these stones to become bread.' Jesus answered, 'It is written: "Man shall not live on bread alone, but on every word that comes from the mouth of God."' Then the devil took him to the holy city and had him stand on the highest point of the temple. 'If you are the Son of God,' he said, 'throw yourself down. For it is written: "He will command his angels concerning you, and they will lift you up in their hands, so that you will not strike your foot against a stone."' Jesus answered him, 'It is also written: "Do not put the Lord your God to the test."' Again, the devil took him to a very high mountain and showed him all the kingdoms of the world and their splendor. 'All this I will give you,' he said, 'if you will bow down and worship me.' Jesus said to him, 'Away from me, Satan! For it is written: "Worship the Lord your God, and serve him only."' Then the devil left him, and angels came and attended him" (Matt. 4:1–11 NIV).

- "He was a murderer from the beginning, not holding to the truth, for there is no truth in him. When he lies, he speaks his native language, for he is a liar and the father of lies" (John 8:44 NIV).

- "Do not conform to the pattern of this world, but be transformed by the renewing of your mind. Then you will be able to test and approve what God's will is—his good, pleasing and perfect will" (Rom. 12:2 NIV).

- "We demolish arguments and every pretension that sets itself up against the knowledge of God, and we take captive every thought to make it obedient to Christ" (2 Cor. 10:5 NIV).

- "Finally, brothers and sisters, whatever is true, whatever is noble, whatever is right, whatever is pure, whatever is lovely, whatever is admirable—if anything is excellent or praiseworthy—think about such things" (Phil. 4:8 NIV).

- "The gatekeeper opens the gate for him, and the sheep listen to his voice. He calls his own sheep by name and leads them out" (John 10:3 NIV).

- "For am I now seeking the approval of man, or of God? Or am I trying to please man? If I were still trying to please man, I would not be a servant of Christ" (Gal. 1:10 ESV).

## Reflection Questions

1. Thought dump: What are your top three negative thoughts?

2. Recognize: What is the theme of your negative thoughts?

3. Replace: What are the three scriptures you can use to replace the lies you believe about yourself?

4. Rewrite: Take time to rewrite your three lies into truths.

5. Recite: Take a moment to speak your rewrites out loud.

6. Repeat: Do you have more negative thoughts? Don't stop this process; keep going. Make this part of your weekly routine.

7. Refuse: What plan can you put in place so you won't give up?

## Chapter 8: The Company You Keep

### Breakthrough Run Through

- When you battle with anxiety, it's important to realize that not everyone is equipped to handle you.

- People can love you well even if they don't understand what you are experiencing.

- Speaking up for yourself is not mean; it's wise.

- You don't have to hide your hardships to make someone else happy.

- Not every problem is yours to solve.

- Advice for overcoming fear and anxiety: TAA (take action always).

- Your pause is your priority.

- You can't hide behind your anxiety as an excuse to not perform, and you can't wear anxiety like a badge of honor.

- Categories of people:

  - Inner circle

  - Pouring

  - Close friends and family

  - Work relationships

  - Convenience

  - Acquaintance

  - Authority

- "Be authentic with all. Transparent with most. Intimate with some." —Beth Moore

- Not everyone in your life gets the privilege of going to the mountaintop with you.

- High places are reserved for high people—the inner circle.

- Within your inner circle, you experience things together that no one else sees, and no one else will understand the experiences but your inner circle.

- When God has blessed you with an inner circle, you recognize it's a privilege to be a part of it. You don't take it for granted, and you often celebrate what God has done in and through your relationships.

- Inner circle people understand how important it is to listen to the voice of God.

- Inner circle relationships equip and encourage you to overcome fear by pointing you back to Jesus.

- You uphold a level of confidentiality within an inner circle that you wouldn't dare dream of destroying.

- "Transparent with most." This works great with the pouring friends, work friends, close friends, and family. When I think of transparency, I think of a glass shower door. Often, it's frosted glass. You can see through it, but you can't see everything.

- Be the same in public as you are in private. When you achieve that, then you are walking in genuine authenticity.

- Three main things are needed when experiencing anxiety—space, comfort, and truth.

- Run to Jesus before you run to anyone else. People cannot solve our fears and anxiety—only God can.

## SCRIPTURES

- "The LORD will fight for you; you need only to be still" (Exod. 14:14 NIV).

- "Six days later Jesus took Peter and the two brothers, James and John, and led them up a high mountain to be alone. As the men watched, Jesus' appearance was transformed so that his face shone like the sun, and his clothes became as white as light. Suddenly, Moses and Elijah appeared and began talking with Jesus.

  Peter exclaimed, 'Lord, it's wonderful for us to be here! If you want, I'll make three shelters as memorials—one for you, one for Moses, and one for Elijah.'

  But even as he spoke, a bright cloud overshadowed them, and a voice from the cloud said, 'This is my dearly loved Son, who brings me great joy. Listen to him.' The disciples were terrified and fell face down on the ground.

  Then Jesus came over and touched them. 'Get up,' he said. 'Don't be afraid.' And when they looked up, Moses and Elijah were gone, and they saw only Jesus.

  As they went back down the mountain, Jesus commanded them, 'Don't tell anyone what you have seen until the Son of Man has been raised from the dead'" (Matt. 17:1–9 NLT).

- "Bad company corrupts good character" (1 Cor. 15:33 NLT).

## Reflection Questions

1. In what ways can people love you even if they don't understand what you are experiencing?

2. Take a current issue creating anxiety in your life, and ask these five questions.

    a.  What specifically is the problem?

    b.  What part of this can I control?

    c.  What part of this can I not control?

    d.  Is this a problem I can solve? If so, do I want to?

    e.  If I can and want to solve the problem, what am I going to do next?

3.  Do you have a hard time speaking up for yourself? Why or why not?

4.  Do you ever hide behind anxiety as an excuse to not carry out your responsibilities? Explain.

5.  In your own words, define the categories of people.

    a.  Inner circle

    b.  Pouring

    c.  Close friends and family

    d.  Work relationships

    e.  Convenience

    f.  Acquaintance

    g.  Authority

6. Discuss how you can "Be authentic with all. Transparent with most. Intimate with some." —Beth Moore

7. What comforts you? Your people can't read your mind, so it's important to let them know what will comfort you.

## Chapter 9: Aftershock

## Breakthrough Run Through

- I often call anxiety setbacks aftershocks.

- When anxiety is caused by our own doing, we must get honest with ourselves and take inventory of our difficulties because anxiety stirred up by sin never leads to peace.

- Here is a short list of questions to ask yourself when trouble comes to determine if you have done something to initiate anxiety:

  - Have I been disobedient to God?

  - Am I holding a grudge or walking in unforgiveness?

  - Am I distant from God?

- His Word is a package deal; surrender to him means submission to the Bible.

- We don't want to have a log in our eye and judge the speck in someone else's. We need to take an honest look at anxiety levels.

- Unforgiveness locks you inside an isolated restless prison.

- It's too costly to hold a grudge.

- Forgiveness does not diminish hurt or pain or give someone permission to keep abusing you.

- Extending forgiveness is not dependent on the other person apologizing.

- Making God our priority is key to overcoming the aftershocks of panic and anxiety.

- Being a Christian does not exempt you from trials; it equips you for them.

- Fear is worse than the trial itself.

- God's grace fills us when we are in our darkest moments.

- Aftershock tips:

  - Don't try to hide it. Denial adds more weight to your already heavy chest.

  - Be kind to yourself. Shaming yourself into believing you are weak, faithless, and worthless only perpetuates the anxiety cycle.

  - The aftermath can leave a mess. Just like an aftershock hitting an area leaves a crumbly mess, so does panic in our bodies.

- Powering through will leave you powerless.

- If we can't give one full day to God, are we trusting him to be God?

## SCRIPTURES

- "But understand this, that in the last days there will come times of difficulty. For people will be lovers of self, lovers of money, proud, arrogant, abusive, disobedient to their parents, ungrateful, unholy, heartless, unappeasable, slanderous, without self-control, brutal, not loving good, treacherous, reckless, swollen with conceit, lovers of pleasure rather than lovers of God, having the appearance of godliness, but denying its power. Avoid such people" (2 Tim. 3:1–5 ESV).

- "But when you are praying, first forgive anyone you are holding a grudge against, so that your Father in heaven will forgive your sins, too" (Mark 11:25 NLT).

- "Draw near to God, and he will draw near to you" (James 4:8 ESV).

- "The thief comes only to steal and kill and destroy; I have come that they may have life, and have it to the full" (John 10:10 NIV).

- "He says, 'Be still, and know that I am God; I will be exalted among the nations, I will be exalted in the earth'" (Psalm 46:10 NIV).

- "Remember the Sabbath day by keeping it holy. Six days you shall labor and do all your work, but the seventh day is a sabbath to the LORD your God. On it you shall not do any work. . . . For in six days the LORD made the heavens and the earth, the sea, and all that is in them, but he rested on the seventh day. Therefore the LORD blessed the Sabbath day and made it holy" (Exod. 20:9–11 NIV).

## Reflection Questions

1. Define what an aftershock is in your own words.

2. Which of these three questions do you struggle with the most? Explain.

   a. Have I been disobedient to God?

   b. Am I holding a grudge or walking in unforgiveness?

   c. Am I distant from God?

3. Read 2 Timothy 3:1–7; what behaviors listed do you struggle with the most?

4. What did you learn about forgiveness? Is there someone in your life whom you are refusing to forgive?

5. How does being a Christian target you for trials?

6. Do you tend to hide or beat yourself up after an aftershock? Explain.

7. Do you currently take one full day off of work to honor the Lord? What steps could you take to start making Sabbath a priority?

## Chapter 10: In This Life, You Will Have Trouble

### Breakthrough Run Through

- As you believe in Jesus more and more, your faith will increase.

- We won't live a fearless life, but we can learn to live more fearlessly.

- Fear surrendered to Jesus brings us peace.

- Every piece of God's armor is crucial if you want to stand firm against the enemy's plans.

  ◆ Belt of truth

  ◆ Breastplate of righteousness

  ◆ Shoes of peace

  ◆ Shield of faith

  ◆ Helmet of salvation

  ◆ Sword of the spirit

  ◆ Prayer

- Prayer is the most potent weapon we have in our arsenal.

- Faith doesn't come with an easy button.

## SCRIPTURES

- "And who can win this battle against the world? Only those who believe that Jesus is the Son of God" (1 John 5:5 NLT).

- "For our struggle is not against flesh and blood, but against the rulers, against the authorities, against the powers of this dark world and against the spiritual forces of evil in the heavenly realms" (Eph. 6:12 NIV).

- "Finally, be strong in the Lord and in his mighty power. Put on the full armor of God, so that you can take your stand against the devil's schemes. For our struggle is not against flesh and blood, but against the rulers, against the authorities, against the powers of this dark world and against the spiritual forces of evil in the heavenly realms. Therefore put on the full armor of God, so that when the day of evil comes, you may be able to stand your ground, and after you have done every-thing, to stand. Stand firm then, with the belt of truth buckled around your waist, with the breastplate of righteousness in place, and with your feet fitted with the readiness that comes from the gospel of peace. In addition to all this, take up the shield of faith, with which you can extinguish all the flam-ing arrows of the evil one. Take the helmet of salvation and the sword of the Spirit, which is the word of God. And pray in the Spirit on all occasions with all kinds of prayers and requests. With this in mind, be alert and always keep on pray-ing for all the Lord's people" (Eph. 6:10–18 NIV).

- "Therefore, my dear friends, as you have always obeyed—not only in my presence, but now much more in my absence—continue to work out your salvation with fear and trembling, for it is God who works in you to will and to act in order to fulfill his good purpose" (Phil. 2:12–13 NIV).

- "For the word of God is alive and active. Sharper than any double-edged sword, it penetrates even to dividing soul and spirit, joints and marrow; it judges the thoughts and attitudes of the heart" (Heb. 4:12 NIV).

- "Don't worry about anything; instead, *pray* about everything. Tell God what you need, and thank him for all he has done. Then you will experience God's peace, which exceeds any-thing we can understand. His peace will guard your hearts and minds as you live in Christ Jesus" (Phil. 4:6–7 NLT—emphasis mine).

- "The testing of [our] faith produces perseverance" (James 1:3 NIV).

- "I have told you these things, so that in me you may have peace. In this world you will have trouble. But take heart! I have overcome the world" (John 16:33 NIV).

## Reflection Questions

1. How has your faith increased through the years?

2. How can surrendering your fears to Jesus bring peace?

3. List the pieces of armor, and define them in your own words.

4. How often do you pray? What steps can you take today to increase prayer in your life?

5. Are you dodging, stopping, or being destroyed by the enemy's bullets? Explain.

6. Why is building your faith hard to do?

## Chapter 11: Wave the White Flag

### Breakthrough Run Through

- Fear is rising because faith is dying.

- Control has us white-knuckling something, and it isn't God.

- Lack of surrender is how we open the door for fear and anxiety to take root.

- Salvation is not surrendering. Salvation is a decision; surrender is an ongoing choice.

- Control is the opposite of surrender.

- Steps of surrender:

- Commit to Jesus
- Commit to building our faith
  - Commit to the Word
  - Commit to prayer
  - Commit to a local church
  - Commit to godly friendships
  - Commit to pursuing healing
- Commit your actions to the Lord
- Commit to discipline
- Commit to letting go of control

- I believe every moment we don't surrender, we allow the enemy to steal precious moments from our life by worrying about things we cannot control.

- There is always an opportunity to worry and always an opportunity to trust God. Which one will you choose?

- Strength is found in surrender.

## SCRIPTURES

- "And it is impossible to please God without faith. Anyone who wants to come to him must believe that God exists and that he rewards those who sincerely seek him" (Heb. 11:6 NLT).

- "And God placed all things under his feet and appointed him to be head over everything for the church, which is his body, the fullness of him who fills everything in every way" (Eph. 1:22–23 NIV).

- "Therefore go and make disciples of all nations, baptizing them in the name of the Father and of the Son and of the Holy Spirit, and teaching them to obey everything I have commanded you. And surely I am with you always, to the very end of the age" (Matt. 28:19–20 NIV).

- "Commit your actions to the LORD, and your plans will succeed" (Prov. 16:3 NLT).

- "God opposes the proud and gives grace to the humble" (James 4:6 ESV).

- "If any of you wants to be my follower, you must give up your own way, take up your cross, and follow me. If you try to hang on to your life, you will lose it. But if you give up your life for my sake, you will save it" (Matt. 16:24–25 NLT).

- "'Abraham! Abraham!'

  'Yes,' Abraham replied. 'Here I am!'

  'Don't lay a hand on the boy!' the angel said. 'Do not hurt him in any way, for now I know that you truly fear God. You have not withheld from me even your son, your only son.'

  Then Abraham looked up and saw a ram caught by its horns in a thicket. So he took the ram and sacrificed it as a burnt offering in place of his son. Abraham named the place Yahweh-Yireh (which means 'the LORD will provide'). To this day, people still use that name as a proverb: 'On the mountain of the LORD it will be provided'" (Gen. 22:11–14 NLT).

- "So don't worry about tomorrow, for tomorrow will bring its own worries. Today's trouble is enough for today" (Matt. 6:34 NLT).

## Reflection Questions

1. Are you yielded to the authority of Jesus Christ? Do any of these statements ring true in your life?

   - I think I can change people.

   - I worry more often than I'm at peace.

   - I like to hover over people and make sure they do things to my expectations.

   - I have a hard time being in the passenger seat.

   - I have confidence in myself but not in others.

   - I trust myself more than I trust God.

   - I often tell people how things will go and leave no room for other options.

   - I rarely consult God.

   - I compare myself to other people.

   - I question the validity of God's Word.

   - I would rather do things myself than ask God for help.

   - I don't think God has my best interest at heart.

   - I control my children because I don't want them to make mistakes.

   - I don't want God's will in my life; I would rather do things my way.

   - I'm confused about my purpose in life.

   - I feel like my plan is the most important.

2. Review the steps of surrender. Which one(s) do you struggle with the most? Explain.

- Commit to Jesus

- Commit to building your faith

  - Commit to the Word

  - Commit to prayer

  - Commit to the local church

  - Commit to godly friendships

  - Commit to pursuing healing

- Commit your actions to the Lord

- Commit to discipline

- Commit to laying down control

3. What are some daily decisions you make without God that you can start pulling him into?

## Chapter 12: Comfort Others with the Comfort You Have Been Given

## Breakthrough Run Through

- Spread comfort like confetti.

- When we follow Jesus, we should look different.

- Your struggle with anxiety is what qualifies you to help.

- When we share our pain and what God has done to meet us in that pain, we glorify him.

- Tools in the hands of God are powerful.

- Your identity is not a personality profile type. Your identity is a child of God, created in the image of God for good works, which he prepared for you before the beginning of time.

### SCRIPTURES

- "He comforts us in all our troubles so that we can comfort others. When they are troubled, we will be able to give them the same comfort God has given us. For the more we suffer for Christ, the more God will shower us with his comfort through Christ. Even when we are weighed down with troubles, it is for your comfort and salvation!" (2 Cor. 1:4–6 NLT).

- "You are the light of the world—like a city on a hilltop that cannot be hidden. No one lights a lamp and then puts it under a basket. Instead, a lamp is placed on a stand, where it gives light to everyone in the house. In the same way, let your good deeds shine out for all to see, so that everyone will praise your heavenly Father" (Matt. 5:14–16 NLT).

- "Carry each other's burdens, and in this way you will fulfill the law of Christ" (Gal. 6:2 NIV).

- "My command is this: Love each other as I have loved you" (John 15:12 NIV).

- "In the same way, let your light shine before others, that they may see your good deeds and glorify your Father in heaven" (Matt. 5:16 NIV).

- "Don't withhold good from someone who deserves it, when it is in your power to do so" (Prov. 3:27 CEB).

- "In everything I have shown you that, by working hard, we must help the weak. In this way we remember the Lord Jesus' words: 'It is more blessed to give than to receive'" (Acts 20:35 NIV).

- "Therefore go and make disciples of all nations, baptizing them in the name of the Father and of the Son and of the Holy Spirit, and teaching them to obey everything I have commanded you. And surely I am with you always, to the very end of the age" (Matt. 28:19–20 NIV).

- Scripture references

    - Spiritual gifts (1 Cor. 12)

    - Leadership (Rom. 12:8)

    - Administration (1 Cor. 12:28)

    - Teaching (1 Cor. 12:28; Rom. 12:7; Eph. 4:11)

    - Words of knowledge (1 Cor. 12:28)

    - Wisdom (1 Cor. 12:28)

    - Prophecy (1 Cor. 12:10; Rom. 12:6)

    - Discernment (1 Cor. 12:10)

    - Exhortation (Rom. 12:8)

    - Shepherding (Eph. 4:11)

    - Faith (1 Cor. 12:9)

    - Evangelism (Eph. 4:11)

    - Apostleship (1 Cor. 12:28; Eph. 4:11)

    - Service/helping (1 Cor. 12:28; Rom. 12:7)

- Mercy (Rom. 12:8)

- Giving (Rom. 12:8)

- Hospitality (1 Pet. 4:9)

## Reflection Questions

1. How does following Jesus set us apart from the world?

2. How can comforting someone else reduce your anxiety?

3. Have you ever believed you have to be panic-free and anxiety-free before you can help someone else with it? If so, why do you think that?

4. How does sharing your pain lead to purpose and glorifying God?

5. Take time to take the spiritual gifts test on Lifeway.com. What are your top five gifts?

6. How can you submit these gifts to God and use them to start comforting someone else?

## Chapter 13: Walk in Freedom

### Breakthrough Run Through

- Being still is not a passive approach; it's the best approach possible.

- Stop striving and let God fight on your behalf; rest in him and surrender.

- Your help comes from the Lord, not from self.

- Hoping for a better tomorrow doesn't do anything, but putting faith in motion does.

- A better life has nothing to do with achievements, success, or material things, but it does have everything to do with surrender and obedience to Jesus Christ.

- This world is not our home. Heaven is.

- The devil can't read your thoughts, but he can hear your words. What are you going to declare today? Faith statements or fear statements?

- God has a clear destiny for you, and it's not a life disrupted by continual fear and annoying anxiety.

## SCRIPTURES

- "Be still, and know that I am God!" (Ps. 46:10 NLT).

- "You are the salt of the earth. But what good is salt if it has lost its flavor? Can you make it salty again? It will be thrown out and trampled underfoot as worthless" (Matt. 5:13 NLT).

- "Bad company corrupts good morals" (1 Cor. 15:33 AMP).

- "In this world you will have trouble" (John 16:33 NIV).

- "Now faith is the substance of things hoped for, the evidence of things not seen" (Heb. 11:1 NKJV).

- "That is why I tell you not to worry about everyday life—whether you have enough food and drink, or enough clothes to wear. Isn't life more than food, and your body more than clothing? Look at the birds. They don't plant or harvest or store food in barns, for your heavenly Father feeds them. And aren't you far more valuable to him than they are? Can all your worries add a single moment to your life?

And why worry about your clothing? Look at the lilies of the field and how they grow. They don't work or make their clothing, yet Solomon in all his glory was not dressed as beautifully as they are. And if God cares so wonderfully for wildflowers that are here today and thrown into the fire tomorrow, he will certainly care for you. Why do you have so little faith?

So don't worry about these things, saying, 'What will we eat? What will we drink? What will we wear?' These things dominate the thoughts of unbelievers, but your heavenly Father already knows all your needs. Seek the Kingdom of God above all else, and live righteously, and he will give you everything you need.

So don't worry about tomorrow, for tomorrow will bring its own worries. Today's trouble is enough for today" (Matt. 6:25–35 NLT).

## Reflection Questions

1. Can you firmly answer that you are following Jesus? How do you know?

2. We are body, soul, and spirit. Are there any parts of your being that are not being cared for properly?

3. What are some ways you can be committed to studying God's love?

4. What step of the five Rs—recognize, replace, recite, repeat, and refuse—do you struggle with the most?

5. Are there any steps you can take today to trust God amid your problems?

6. Are you entirely surrendered to Jesus? How do you know?

7. How can you use your story for God's glory?

# Ready Statements

- I will not trust my insight; instead, I will walk in God's wisdom. (Adapted from Proverbs 28:26)

- I will not be conformed to the patterns of this world but be transformed by the renewing of my mind. (Adapted from Romans 12:2)

- I lift my eyes up; my help comes from God. (Adapted from Psalm 121:1–2)

- I do not operate out of the spirit of fear because God has given me a sound mind. (Adapted from 2 Timothy 1:7)

- I will not be afraid, for God is close beside me. His rod and staff protect and comfort me. (Adapted from Psalm 23:4)

- I will not walk in fear; I will walk in God's love. (Adapted from 1 John 4:18)

- I will not fail; God is within me. (Adapted from Psalm 46:5)

- I declare this about the Lord: He alone is my refuge, my place of safety; he is my God, and I trust him. (Adapted from Psalm 91:2)

- I will take time to rest and be with God alone. (Adapted from Mark 6:30–32)

- I will live at peace with everyone as far as it depends on me. (Adapted from Romans 12:18)

- I am valuable. (Adapted from Luke 12:7)

- I am forgiven. (Adapted from Psalm 103:10–12)

- I will love you, Lord, with all my heart, soul, and mind. (Adapted from Matthew 22:37)

- I will not listen to the enemy's lies. (Adapted from John 8:44)

- I will demolish arguments and every pretension that sets itself up against the knowledge of God and take captive every thought to make it obedient to Christ. (Adapted from 2 Corinthians 10:5)

- I will not seek the approval of man. (Adapted from Galatians 1:10)

- I will not be corrupted by bad company; I will surround myself with godly people. (Adapted from 1 Corinthians 15:33)

- I will draw near to God, and he will draw near to me. (Adapted from James 4:8)

- I will be still and trust God. (Adapted from Psalm 46:10)

- I will be strong in the Lord, and I will put on the whole armor of God every day. (Adapted from Ephesians 6)

- I will work out my salvation with fear and trembling. (Adapted from Philippians 2:12–13)

- I will not worry about anything but instead, pray about everything. (Adapted from Philippians 4:6)

- I will have peace in God. (Adapted from John 16:33)

- I will go and make disciples. (Adapted from Matthew 28:19)

- I will shine my light bright for Jesus. (Adapted from Matthew 5:14–16)